SUPERCONSCIOUS
MEDITATION

SUPERCONSCIOUS MEDITATION

Kundalini

and the

Understanding of the Whole Mind

Daniel R. Condron
D.M., D.D., M.S.

SOM Publishing
Windyville, Missouri 65783 U.S.A.

© August, 1998
by the School of Metaphysics No. 100161

Cover Art by Sharka Glet & Hezekiah Daniel Condron

ISBN: 0-944386-21-0

Library of Congress Catalogue Number pending

PRINTED IN THE UNITED STATES OF AMERICA

If you desire to learn more about the research and
teachings in this book, write to School of Metaphysics,
World Headquarters, Windyville, Missouri 65783.
Or call us at 417-345-8411.
Visit us on the Internet at www.som.org

Foreword

I suppose everyone wants peace, both peace of Mind and peace within the world. World peace begins with people creating peace within themselves. You do not find peace. You create peace.

To master any skill or ability, practice is required. To master meditation, you will need to meditate regularly. To become proficient, you will want and need to meditate everyday.

Meditation is the art of stilling the Mind and listening. In the stillness you will know your permanent, everlasting existence. You will come to know this in this life.

The essence of meditation is in receiving from the inner Self. You will learn, in meditation, to draw upon resources, knowledge, wisdom, and understanding that you did not previously know existed within yourself.

My more than twenty years of experience meditating and teaching others to meditate has shown me that everyone can benefit from meditation. When you don't meditate you may have some good days and some bad days. When you meditate every day, more and more you will have good days. Things seem to go right for you. You are centered and purposeful in life. You understand your purpose in life more and more each day and you lead a fulfilling, satisfying and growthful life.

You are on this earth for a reason. This reason will become increasingly apparent to you as you meditate every day. Your friendships will increase, deepen, and be enhanced. In meditation, your consciousness will expand to all of Creation. This book is about all of these benefits of meditation and much more. This book explains to you exactly what the Mind is, how it works, and how you can harness it for your benefit and fulfillment. Meditation is to be your tool, your vehicle for accomplishing this great task, which will also be your greatest joy.

Everything you ever imagined becoming and creating becomes possible with meditation.

You are important. You are valuable. You have a potential greatness within yourself. It is just waiting to be drawn out. This book offers you insight, direction, and help in making the journey to Self awareness, Self knowledge, Self understanding and finally enlightenment.

Daniel R. Condron

Contents

It was time for our annual National Teacher's Conference. We all gathered around the long tables, anxiously waiting to find out more about our dreams and to receive wisdom from Dr. Daniel Condron. It seemed as though the common theme or the message from our dreams revolved around being open and learning about our emotions. I was listening intently as Dr. Daniel Condron began to open himself up and give, helping us all to understand how to reveal ourselves, how to learn more, helping us to learn about our emotions and how to use them for their intended purpose, and on and on. Just then I looked over at him and there was this pinkish-orange circle that turned into gold as it spun round and round, faster and faster, shooting out rays of golden light emanating from his heart area. The golden rays shot out and connected to each individual. It was so beautiful of an experience. This wave of energy flowed through me and out the top of my head. Tears welled up in my eyes, causing the light to now glisten as it poured out of him. It was then that I knew how important what he was saying was to each one of us at this time. Flashes of images revealed themselves to me as I continued to listen, like a motion picture. As he closed the session, I was left with a deep love that was shared with each on this morning. I was grateful for this cherished experience. I also knew there would be more. I thought how privileged we all were to witness this and to have the blessing of sharing with others this magnificent light and love that I believe will continue to live on and on in us all.

Teresa Padilla
April 5, 1998

Introduction

In this book I have combined two ideas: meditation and the Mind.

When I use the word Mind I do not mean just the Conscious Mind nor do I mean the brain which is a physical organ. The Conscious Mind is only one division of Mind. The individual's conscious mind works with the five senses of sight, smell, hearing, taste, and touch. When I use the word Mind I am referring to the whole Mind which consists of the Conscious, Subconscious, and Superconscious Minds.

Meditation requires that you use your mind to go deeper and deeper within. The ultimate goal is to expand your consciousness beyond Mind and know I AM. When the Self that is you has expanded or grown beyond Mind then you have also transcended space and time. Space and time are functions of the vehicle called Mind.

Mind is the vehicle you will use to know Self. It is good to meditate. It is even better when you know how to meditate correctly. It is still better when you are aware of the roads and obstacles that exist on way to Self understanding. You need to learn how to use the vehicle of the Mind in order to gain Self understanding.

You are on this earth for a purpose. That purpose you can discover, in and through meditation.

Although there is much information in this book always remember that in its simplest, most basic form or level, meditation is and may be defined as: stilling the mind, directing the attention inward and listening. Therefore, learn to still your mind.

Concentration exercises aid in improving the listening ability and are therefore discussed in this book. Mental discipline is important also in stilling the mind and is presented in this book. Those tools of the Mind necessary for Self understanding and Self awareness are presented herein.

Each chapter includes questions about meditation and the Mind that I have been asked by my students. I have been asked most of these questions many times. I have found them to be the kinds of questions that students of meditation *universally* ask. I believe they will help to answer some of your questions about meditation.

In each chapter you will read about the meditation experiences of others. These are the meditation experiences of my students. They are included for the reader's education and also for motivation. You must be motivated to meditate. By reading of other students' successes in meditation it is my hope that the desire for the benefits of meditation will be kindled even stronger within yourself.

It is my profound desire that you come to know your purpose in life and to know who you are.

I have meditated for over 20 years now and I can tell you the benefits are great. However, you do not have to wait 20 years to gain the benefits of meditation. The moment you still your mind and sit quietly you begin to gain benefits. As you learn to direct your attention within, the benefits of meditation increase. You begin to gain an inner glow as the inner knowledge comes pouring into your consciousness.

I know you are ready for more rapid soul growth and spiritual development. This is why you are reading this book right now.

When truth is accepted into the conscious mind often there is a welling up of tears from the joyful emotion that has been experienced. For as truth is accepted in the outer Self the truth from the inner Self finds a worthy receptacle. The conscious mind that has accepted truth is in a receptive and receiving mode. The conscious or outer mind is thereby made capable of receiving from the inner Subconscious and Superconscious mind.

When the conscious or outer waking mind is receptive then the truth that is in the process of manifesting into your outer waking life can move through the emotional level of consciousness. Emotions of joy and happiness are a good sign that your desires are moving from the inner or Subconscious mind into your outer physical, waking, life.

A still or quiet mind makes all of this possible. For with the still mind all divisions of mind: Conscious, Subconscious, and Superconscious are aligned, thereby enabling the thinker to have full access to the inner Subconscious and Superconscious minds.

When the conscious mind is stilled you are no longer a victim of time. No longer do you feel that time is running out. Physical time is a product of physical existence. The sun rises in the morning and 24 hours later the sun rises again. We call this one day. The earth revolves around the sun and we call one complete revolution a year. In Subconscious mind we

Why Meditate?

Meditate because meditation improves every area
and every part of your life.
Meditate because it is good for you.
Meditate because it will fulfill you.
Meditate because you need to find your purpose for this
lifetime.
Meditate so you can have more good to offer others.
Meditate so you can gain the higher knowledge, wisdom,
and enlightenment.
Meditate so you can offer knowledge, wisdom,
and enlightenment to others.
Meditate so you may become compatible to your Creator.
Meditate so you may enter the inner levels of consciousness
with awareness.
Meditate so that you may overcome sadness, depression,
anger, greed, jealousy, envy, resentment, hatred, insecurity, and
low Self worth.
Meditate because it is the most fulfilling, rewarding, thing
you can do. In meditation you may experience love
and you will be filled with Light.
Meditate so that each day will go well for you.
Meditate so that each day you will feel and be
centered and aligned.
Meditate so you will be a better husband or wife.
Meditate so you will be a better friend.
Meditate so you may form deeper friendships.
Meditate so you may know God.
Meditate so you may experience the Creator.
Meditate so you will expand your consciousness.
Meditate so you will be happy.
Meditate because change
is the greatest competence one can acquire.
Meditate
to enable you to change and grow easily, and rapidly.

don't have minutes, hours, days, and years. In Subconscious mind we measure time according to the permanent learning, called understandings, that we have accumulated. This is vertical time. Horizontal or physical time is measured according to movement from one physical place to another. The minute hand of a clock revolves once in an hour. The earth rotates once in a 24 hour day, creating our day length.

Physical time is limited. A physical lifetime extends a few years or a few decades on earth while vertical time, Superconscious time, is eternal. When you identify with and operate from vertical time you have an eternity to accomplish all your needs. You are no longer limited by time.

You need to realize that you can determine the conditions of your life consciously. Meditation enables you to do so. Meditation is a form of Self discipline. Both Self discipline and discipline of the mind are the keys to knowledge.

Everyone needs to have a belief in a significance in their lives, a significance that involves more than just the Self. The significance to the life must involve lots of other people, thereby one expands the level of giving to others and all humanity. It is through giving that one will discover the greatest significance one is seeking. Meditation is perhaps the greatest gift you can give to yourself. Through meditation past understandings are awakened and you connect the day-to-day physical activities with the greater purpose or spiritual awareness of the Self.

You need to cultivate a positive expectation in meditation. You need to have a strong belief and conviction that when you ask a question that you want answered in meditation that it will be answered. The answer may or may not come as in a voice whispering or yelling in your ear. The answer may come later in the day when you know the right decision to make or the correct thing to do.

When you are preparing for meditation, remember that your mind is to be focused. The mind is to be directed and concentrated. All thoughts should depart as the mind is focused upon listening for the answer to your prayer.

Concentration is not constricting. Concentration is an easy flow and movement of energy. Therefore when concentration is applied to meditation, the flow of energy from the inner Self to the outer physical self is facilitated.

Love is an excellent word to receive insight about during meditation.

Meditating upon love is the key to a person fulfilling desires of the Self. Love removes the selfishness, the greed, and the taking thoughts and attitudes from a person. In their place, love offers free giving, free and open receiving, caring, concern, friendliness, joy, happiness, abundance, and prosperity. When one is giving freely, without restriction, then the mind and Self are free to receive from the bounties of the Universe. The Universe has no limitations.

Meditation also helps a person to change. Most everyone has something about the Self they would like to change. Perhaps you are not a good public speaker and would like to improve, perhaps you are afraid to tell people that you love them, perhaps you have low Self worth and would like to build Self value; these you can change and achieve and much more. When considering change, focus on a positive ideal rather than something to fight against or get rid of. When you are fighting against something or someone in your mind you are closed off to receiving. As long as you are closed off to receiving and have walls of protection around the Self, you will be unable to receive from Superconscious Mind the answer to your prayers. You will not even be able to receive from your Subconscious Mind.

Meditation is aligning the whole Self with Creation and Creator.

The reason it is important to meditate is that meditation is the tool that allows one to overcome physical entrapment, engrossment, and limitations. It enables you to contact and gradually or quickly come to know the Real Self.

Meditation provides many benefits to people that are not available to the average person. Meditation can reduce stress, provide peace of mind, and calmness. In addition, the person who meditates regularly will, over time, gain a greater sense of purpose in his or her life. In fact, through meditation one can discover his or her purpose and assignment in life.

Some people think they exist in this lifetime to make money or to have children. While these may be valuable goals they are neither the sole nor main reason we exist in this physical world and in a physical body.

One of the first realizations you may have in meditation is that you are not the physical body. You are a soul existing in a physical body. Your physical body is a vehicle that you, a soul, use to carry you through a lifetime. A physical body is like a suit of clothes that you, a soul, put on at the beginning of a lifetime. You wear this fine suit of clothes, your body, throughout a lifetime, and when it is worn out at the end of a lifetime, you discard it. Your soul, however, the real you, who has worn the clothing-body for a lifetime continues to exist.

The real you, your inner Self is eternal. The physical body is temporary. Through the use of meditation you, the thinker are able to contact and identify with your Real Self, the soul. The physical body is limited. The soul, the real you is eternal. Through meditation you will learn to be in constant communion with your High Self, your Real Self, the Eternal and Permanent You.

By meditating regularly, you identify less and less with frustrations, limitations, irritations, re-actions, angers, fears, doubts, worries, guilts, jealousies, and all such restrictions. Instead you will come more and more to align yourself with freedom which is the native condition of the soul. I do not mean freedom from responsibility. Rather you will gain the freedom to create and become a creator. Response-ability or respond-ability is freedom or it is the ability to respond to the real needs and desires of the Real Self.

You will never be happy, truly and deeply happy, until you learn to know your inner Self. Meditation enables you to first believe there is a greater significance to life and an expectation to find it rather than doubt you will ever find or have it. Consistent and dedicated meditation proves this to you and you come to know your great purpose and mission in life. This one step alone will change your life in a tremendous way for the better.

Complete relaxation and conscious withdrawal of the attention from the five senses is the only way to go deep into Mind to know I AM. The attention must be removed from the physical body and the five senses. In deep meditation, your consciousness expands to fill the whole universe.

The whole body changes when you meditate frequently and regularly; all the way down to your DNA. Intuitive Man's DNA will be different and more evolved than Reasoning Man's DNA. Meditation means constantly thinking of the vastness all around you and encompassing the whole universe so the Self will forget its attachment to a limited physical body and remember the unlimited, all expansive Self.

Meditation overcomes fears. Most people have fears. Then they adopt a strategy for coping with the fear. From this strategy of coping with the fear they create a limiting attitude that causes re-actions and dis-ease. Instead they need to come to terms with and understand the truth in order to go beyond the fear.

Regular meditation causes there to be more clarity in the thinking. With greater clarity in the thinking you are able to make better decisions with fewer mistakes. You are able to reason out the answers to the deeper questions you have about yourself and about life. Meditation heightens your awareness of your reason for existence. You need to use your meditation time in the quest to understand the total Self and the High Self.

The practice of meditation will provide the awareness of one's connection and unity with what is eternal, what is permanent, and what is more than and beyond the physical existence.

Death is the permanent withdrawal of the attention from the physical body. In order to go to heaven after death you must learn to experience and cause heaven on earth. In other words you need to learn to experience Superconscious Mind while you are incarned in a physical body this lifetime in order to experience Superconscious Mind after the end of this lifetime. Since heaven or Superconscious Mind is not somewhere afar such as Mars or Jupiter but rather is everywhere at all times and always near us we must learn to create heaven on earth. Each person needs to cause there to be heaven on earth.

When a person causes there to be heaven on earth and perfectly reflects and lives the seed idea of perfection and enlightenment held in Superconscious Mind then at the end of a lifetime with the shedding of a physical body comes no cessation of consciousness. Instead Superconscious awareness and existence in heaven, both being the same thing, continue unabated.

In your waking state, your attention is in the conscious mind. The conscious mind works directly with the brain and five senses. When you meditate you learn to still the conscious mind and learn to listen consciously, or with awareness, to the subconscious mind. After learning to harmonize the conscious and subconscious minds, and learning to use both to attain maximum growth for Self, the two minds are attuned to the Superconscious Mind and Cosmic, Buddha, or Christ Consciousness is attained.

The final step of mankind's growth is then to align all three divisions of mind and to know, I AM.

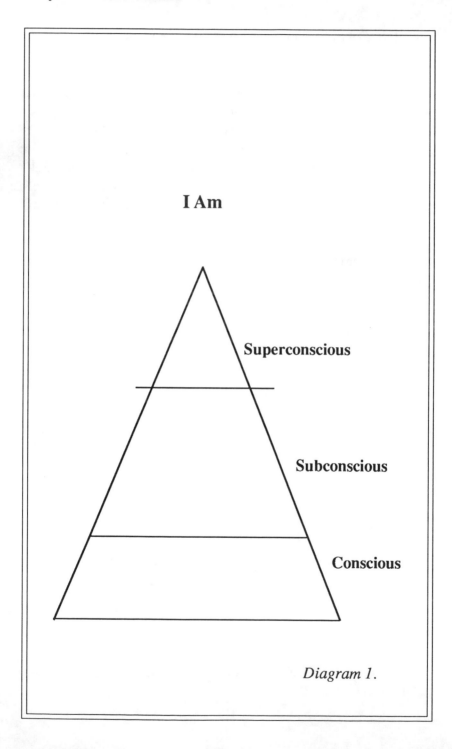

I Am

Superconscious

Subconscious

Conscious

Diagram 1.

Superconscious Meditation

Kundalini
and the
Understanding of the Whole Mind

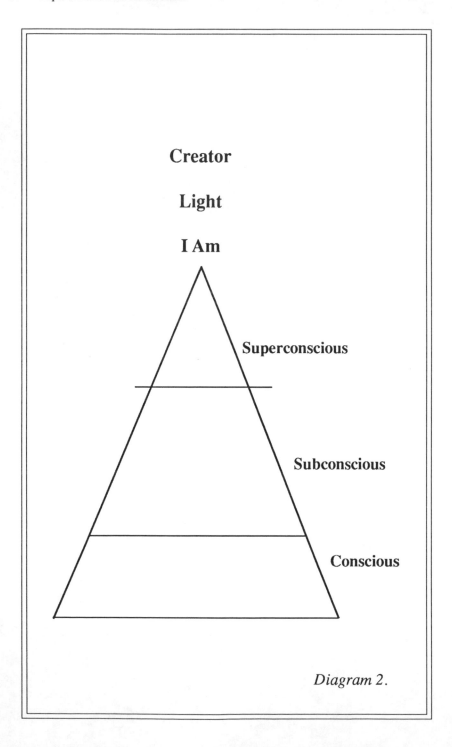

Creator

Light

I Am

Superconscious

Subconscious

Conscious

Diagram 2.

Chapter One

What is I Am and what is Mind ?

Time, space, and the whole mind can be understood and realized in deepening meditation. Any limiting concepts are transcended. In the place of limitations come joy, happiness, exhilaration, peace, and LIGHT.

During a recent Spiritual Initiation Session on the 1500 acre College of Metaphysics campus in the beautiful Ozark Mountains of Southern Missouri, one young woman transcended her previous beliefs about herself, time, and experience.

> *I attended a Spiritual Initiation Session on finding your purpose in life. There were several people there, and one large group meditation.*
>
> *I sat in a peaceful, tranquil state - something I was experiencing for the first time. I saw mostly black, but had no care in the world. I lost track of physical time, I was merely dwelling in a new kind of state of love and peace.*
>
> *I had the freedom to think what I wanted, when I wanted, and the security to know I was at a different place within my Self than I ever experienced before. I didn't care to stop meditating, I probably could have stayed for hours.*
>
> *When I finally did decide to come out of meditating, I had meditated for one and a half hours - my record time. It was exhilarating.*

Meditation causes the minds to align. It is the capacity to listen for the answer to our prayers.

Meditation is quieting the body, stilling the mind, and attuning it to superconsciousness. It is the means by which we come to know who we are.

Meditation fosters spiritual growth, leading to enLIGHTenment. It is soothing, revealing, nurturing, transcendent, and as Traci – the student who is finding her purpose in life – discovered exhilarating.

Mind is the vehicle I AM uses to experience in and through. Mind is the schoolroom or place of learning for the individualized units of LIGHT known as I AM.

In the beginning of Creation the Creator had a great idea, a new awareness, a bright idea, what we call LIGHT. Following this LIGHT of awareness the Creator created individualized units of LIGHT called I Am (plural I AMs).

I AM needed a place to experience and learn. Therefore, Mind was created. At first the Superconscious Mind was created, then the Subconscious Mind and lastly the Conscious Mind. The physical universe we experience primarily with the outer Conscious Mind.

The Mind is made up of three major divisions *(see Diagram 2)*. Notice from the Mind triangle diagram that originally I AM was located and existed above and beyond Mind. Mind is the residence of time and space. Therefore, I AM is beyond time and space.

The ETERNAL Creator exists beyond time and space as do all those fully enlightened beings who have evolved beyond the whole or entire Mind. These are the beings who have become compatible with their Creator. They have become full-fledged helpmates for the Creator in helping or aiding his Creation to come to fruition. These helpmates are causing a quickening of the Creator's Creation in order that mental, emotional, physical, and spiritual evolution may progress more rapidly and mankind may progress into communion with our Creator.

These are the highly evolved entities who have seen God face to face and yet live. They have even gone beyond this to attain a Oneness of consciousness and purpose. These are the enlightened beings who no longer need to re-incarn into a physical body. They have lifted themselves above and beyond the cycle of re-incarnation and karma. They have transcended the limitations of physical existence. These enlightened individuals continually send forth their light and love to all mankind aiding in the quickening of the evolution of the planet.

Just as a child begins his education with the parents so I AM began education with the Creator. Just as children often go to grade school and progress up the higher steps of learning to college or university so I AM entered Mind to learn in the field of experience.

Just as an adolescent or young adult leaves home and goes to college to be taught by older people with more education so do the determined, committed, and highly developed people desire, search for, and find the College of Higher Spiritual learning, illumination, awareness, and enlightenment.

Sometimes I am asked, "If everyone is an I AM then why are we so different?" The answer is that different experiences create different opportunities for learning. Incarning in a female body provides a different type or quality of learning than does choosing to incarn in a male body. Choosing to incarn in the country of China provides different learning than incarning in the United States or France.

In addition, each person uses an experience for different degrees of learning. One person may go through an experience and learn nothing continuing to exist in the same manner until forced to change by the school of hard knocks. Another person can go through the same experience, learn much and be totally transformed to the point that his life is never the same again.

Different experiences and different levels of soul learning based on past and present desire to learn, grow, and gain in Soul awareness, produce differences between individuals both in their personality and in their level of permanent understandings.

I AM plus *experience* plus *reasoning and learning* equals *what makes one person different from another.*

The first creation of the Creator was LIGHT. Following this creation individualized units of LIGHT or I AM were created. This individualized unit of LIGHT or I AM is at the essence of our being. It is what Moses saw in the burning bush. Upon being told by God that he was to tell Pharaoh to let my people go, Moses said, "Who shall I say sent me?" Yahweh (God) speaking through the burning bush said, "Tell him I AM that I AM" *(Bible, Exodus 2)*. Hindus make the statement I AM THAT, which has a similar meaning.

I AM is an individualized unit of light existing beyond time and space. Albert Einstein reached to understand this area beyond time and space in his General Theory of Relativity in which he produced the formula *space · time = matter · energy,* and later when he attempted the Grand Unification Theory or Theory of Everything.

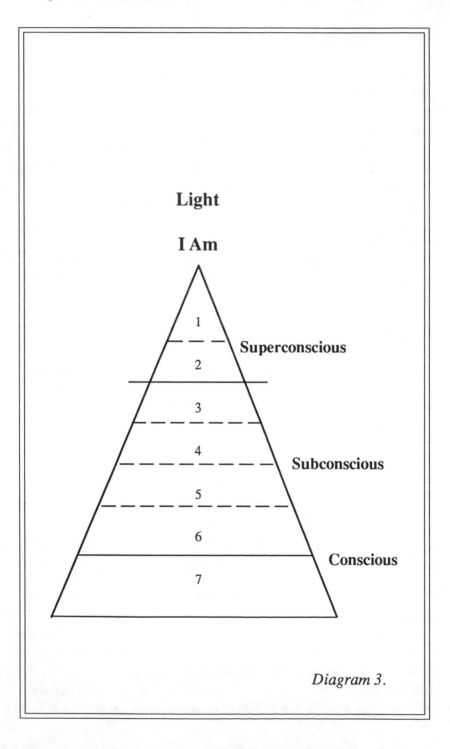

Light

I Am

1

- - - - - Superconscious

2

3

4

- - - - - - - - Subconscious

5

6

Conscious

7

Diagram 3.

I AM, the individualized LIGHT, needed a place to experience in order to learn, grow, and gain understandings. This would enable each I AM to mature as a creator and become compatible to his Creator. For this reason Mind was created. Mind was created in order for I AM to have a vehicle to learn with, to experience in and through.

The seven levels of Mind are seven grades of learning. An analogy may be drawn to the levels of childhood schooling such as the American twelve grades of school. Each offers a place of learning appropriate for the level of awareness one is existing on or at *(see Diagram 3)*.

At the present period in humanity's evolution mankind's attention is engrossed in the five senses and physical experiencing while entrapped in a physical body. Between lifetimes the physical body is released, the soul is free from its entrapment and thereby exists in Subconscious Mind. After death or permanent withdrawal from the physical body the soul begins to assimilate the permanent learning of Creation gained in that lifetime. The assimilation process includes the learning that was gained in the areas of Creation, Universal Laws and Universal Truths. Only those experiences and learning having to do with what is universal are retained. The negativity, fears, greed, doubt, hatred, guilt, and so forth are sloughed off as they are not, and will not become, a part of the permanent Self.

This process of assimilation begins with the sixth level of mind, the Emotional level which is the level of mind closest to the physical. It then proceeds to the fifth, fourth, and third levels in that order. At the completion of this assimilation process the soul has incorporated the permanent understandings gained from that previous lifetime into the whole Self. These newly incorporated understandings are categorized and put in their proper place in relation to understandings gained from previous lifetimes. Then it is known by the soul what areas of understanding are still lacking in the Self and what areas remain to be fulfilled.

Based on this current and up to date data, the soul operating from the third level of mind, the highest or deepest point in Subconscious Mind, begins to determine the circumstances, conditions, factors and assignment for the next upcoming lifetime.

The soul has needs. The soul's needs are for learning and growth that produce understanding of what it is to be a creator. To state it negatively, if experience does not entail learning about Creation, Universal Laws, and Universal Truths, then it does not become an understanding within Self.

Meditation enables the process of the assimilation of permanent understandings to be accelerated. The successful meditator actually quickens this spiritual evolution not only while sitting down and meditating but also by using the alignment of minds gained in meditation to facilitate the building of permanent understanding in the daily life.

The alignment, insight, and awareness gained in meditation must be applied in the daily life in order that a person may create using Universal Laws and Truths.

Between lifetimes one not only assimilates but integrates the accumulated learning from the previous lifetime. Between lifetimes the soul (Self) consolidates the understandings of Self and Creation.

After determining the theme or assignment of the next, upcoming lifetime, the soul, that is you, begins to move from the third level to the fourth level of Mind. Here the ideas of the upcoming lifetime become clearer and firmer.

From the fourth level of Mind the soul moves to the fifth level. Here the thoughts of the upcoming lifetime begin to crystallize, taking on form. The plan-idea-ideal receives substance into itself and thereby becomes firmer and firmer.

In the fifth level of Mind the next lifetime is set. The soul is not only committed to the ideal of the upcoming lifetime, but is also committed to a particular set of physical circumstances. For example, by the time the soul reaches the fifth level in the movement outward into the physical birth of incarnation certain decisions or choices have been made. The country and time period in which one is to incarn have been determined.

The incarning soul chooses the parents and family he or she is to incarn into. The physical mother and father have been narrowed down to one or two possibilities with one choice holding priority. The second choice only being used if there is a miscarriage on the part of the first couple or inability to conceive and become pregnant. In other words the second choice is used only when the opportunity to use the first choice is not available.

As one learns to go deep in meditation into Subconscious Mind one learns to direct the energies in Subconscious Mind before they manifest physically. In fact, learning the art and practice of visualization enables one to use mental picturing or imaging and will power to learn to direct this process of the movement of thought or thought-forms from the physical or Conscious Mind to the deepest level of Subconscious Mind called the Mental or third level of Mind. From the third level of Mind the thought-form moves from fourth, to fifth, to sixth, and finally into the seventh level of Mind. Each movement can be directed by one who has learned to gain access to the Subconscious Mind.

The process of physical death of the body, the movement into Subconscious Mind and back out again is similar to the process a desire or thought-form goes through in moving from Conscious Mind to Subconscious Mind and back to the physical once again as the manifestation of one's desires.

Learning to manifest your desires through the use of visualization aids you in understanding the process of the movement of energies from Conscious Mind to Subconscious Mind to the physical and the new Conscious Mind. This is the process of life and death and the cycle of re-incarnation.

The one who meditates regularly comes to understand this movement of energies and mind substance from one level of Mind to another. He comes to understand the cycle of the movement of energies between the Conscious and Subconscious Minds.

Meditation aligns the minds and causes them to work together in harmony. Thereby, everything in one's life becomes more efficient and easier. The action of dying becomes easier. The action of physical living becomes easier and more efficient. The awareness between lifetimes becomes greater.

The average, physically-engrossed person has very little awareness after physical death and in the intervening period between lifetimes. Such a person drifts in a kind of dreamy sleep, awakening at times to the actions in Subconscious Mind, memories of what they were doing in the previous lifetime. For instance, if that person was a baker he will continue to bake bread between lifetimes. If he was a typist he will continue to type. A banker will continue to bank never realizing he or she is no longer in the physical level of existence. Without the realization that the outer Self has ceased to be, has died, and the inner Self has withdrawn its attention from the physical existence there is little freedom to pursue whatever learning is needed by the soul.

Over a long period of somewhat wasted time such a person is obliged to release that attachment to that previous life in order to move forward in the assimilation process thereby beginning to prepare for the next, upcoming lifetime.

The spiritualized being, the one who meditates consistently and regularly at least once a day, finds the ability to release the physical body at the end of a lifetime easy and painless. It is a choice. The meditator finds he remains conscious after the point of withdrawal or death. He is able to move swiftly through the assimilation process in Subconscious Mind because he has greater Self awareness and awareness of Mind. Such people have developed this awareness while still in the physical lifetime. They have practiced just these things in the most recent lifetime.

Ed is such a person. A Chicago bartender, it would be a surprise to many people that Ed is even interested in spiritual development and peace of mind, but when you've been in that environment you get a heavy dose of the ills that plague us. For each person having fun, looking for love, and just meeting friends there is at least one who is depressed, lonely, with nowhere else to go. Ed's search for awareness through daily meditation helped him keep stability in his own life and lend some to others he met every day.

As a student in the School of Metaphysics he was learning how to relax the body and still the mind in progressive stages. Shortly after entering the second series of lessons, Ed experienced this:

I had just received instruction in the deepening of meditation that would enable me to remove my attention from the outer world and transfer it to the inner levels of mind.

I remember losing some consciousness, then regaining it as I looked at a cloud of orange. I observed it for a while, then asked myself "where's my body?" This startled me and I went back into my body. There was a tingling sensation in my body at that moment. I was thrilled to think that I had just left my body.

I believe I was out of body because the feeling was of lightness, of just being, of great peace. As I brought my attention back to the physical, there was a feeling of heaviness, relative to the experience described.

Leaving the physical body is an experience many people have when they learn to meditate. They find out from their direct experience that they are not the physical body. The physical body is a vehicle that houses the soul during a lifetime. As long as the person is engrossed in his five senses of seeing, touching, tasting, smelling, and hearing, and attached to his physical body that person will never *know* he is a soul.

He may think he is nothing more than a physical body with a limited lifetime restricted to only 70 or 80 years. He may think he has a soul and read of other people's out-of-body experiences or of their experiences of their consciousness expanding beyond their physical body, but only when he actually does it himself will he *know* this truth.

As your consciousness expands beyond your physical body, you do experience greater peace because you are closer to God. As you look at the mind triangle, you will notice that it is wider at the bottom and narrows to a point at the top. The wide bottom of the mind triangle chart symbolizes the scattering of attention that occurs in the Conscious Mind while engrossed in physical experiences. As the meditator learns to still the mind, the thoughts of worry, doubt, fear, anger, resentment and limitation begin to disappear. In the place of these limiting thoughts, the expansion of consciousness begins to make itself known. Instead of the wide separation of sides as is indicated at the bottom of the triangle, there begins to be singular attention and singular ideal as symbolized by the narrowing of the triangle at the top. Finally, at the peak of the triangle the two sides come together indicating the meditator has achieved singular attention and singular ideal and purpose with a lifetime dedicated to learning and growth and service to mankind.

When this is achieved, the thinker's consciousness includes all of creation and he or she knows, I AM.

The awareness of the inner levels of Mind gained in a lifetime is retained. Such a one has access to the inner level spiritual teachers who guide and aid one in the assimilation process and in preparing for the next lifetime. The meditator then is, in effect, preparing for a fortunate rebirth.

As the Conscious Mind is disciplined and comes more and more under the control of the thinker, the Self gains greater freedom to receive from one's Subconscious Mind the permanent understandings one has stored there.

In the final analysis, change is the expansion of consciousness. Most people see change as painful because they wait for things to happen which basically means you turn over the control of your life to your environment. As long as the Conscious Mind is habitual and existing in old memories you see or view the world as you are with your limitations. When you quiet and still your mind you begin to perceive the world as it is which is limitless.

Dr. Barbara Condron often tells of a profound meditation experience that occurred within her first year of spiritual practice.

It was 1976. I had been studying metaphysics for less than a year, and finding the truths personally and universally applicable. I was eager to introduce others to the study and pass on the benefits of spiritual discipline to others. My efforts in these areas brought me to the attention of the leadership of the School of Metaphysics which was in need of a director in the only out-of-state center in Wichita, Kansas.

I remember quite vividly it was Easter weekend. After work on Friday, I spent most of the weekend at the School as had become my custom. I enjoyed the vibratory energy of the center, loved the company and fellowship, and knew I would always learn – through the interactions with others and in activities pursued – things that would deepen my awareness. This particular weekend the president of SOM paid an unannounced visit to our center. Early on Saturday he didn't ask me if I wanted to direct a school. He told me the school needed someone in Wichita and he asked if I would be willing to move there. He said I could think about it and give him an answer before he left on Monday morning.

The opportunity put me in a tailspin. At least it got my imagination going in high gear. The next 30 or so hours were filled with a stream of thoughts all relative to the need to give an answer that I could do more than live with, that I would want to live with.

At 22 and a recent college graduate, my thoughts moved from "what will my parents think" to "how can I leave my friends" to "what about the students I had just started in classes here" to *"what about the lease on my apartment, my job, my possessions."* All the physical considerations, the inconvenience it would cause in responsibly closing my life in one place and beginning a new one elsewhere.

The need to start over – new friends, new students, new source of income – was unsettling because it was not my forte and I would be going alone. All the emotional considerations, the feelings of loss of friendship, the anxiety of what others might think, be it good or bad, the releasing of attachments. The mental struggle, should I, shouldn't I, can I, can't I, if I do will it be the right thing or turn out as my well-meaning critics portend? By Sunday evening I was exhausted, unresolved, and just wanted the whole thing to go away.

Yet the worst was yet to come.

Since I had gained eligibility to attend, I had always been a part of Healing Class. I relished this time of giving, for I realized the projecting of healing energy, in most cases to people I did not know and would never meet, was one of the purest expressions of unconditional love I have ever been privileged to be a part of. Through the many months of healing, I had grown quite proficient in assessment and balancing of energies.

This evening we had a large number of healing requests, ten or eleven, so the healing took over an hour. Following the projection I excused myself from the discussion which always followed the class. I was exasperated with myself. Throughout the healing session I was constantly battling myself, fighting to keep my attention on the task at hand, the person who needed my help. Constantly, my mind was off on some imaginary scenario caused by and fueled by my indecision – was I going or was I not? I knew I wanted to say yes, and I also knew I had all these reasons to say no.

Frustrated I went upstairs, sat in a dark room, and sought peace that I had learned comes in meditation.

My prayer was for peace of mind so I could know the right thing to do. As I prepared my body and mind to enter meditation, I felt the layers of doubt and fear I had allowed to persist *and even encouraged the last hours melt away. They dropped like veils away from the inner light which grew within me, bringing calmness and a familiar comforting joy I had learned to expect when in the proper frame of mind. I don't know how much time passed, but at some point I heard a voice say "Exodus 3:2". It was as if someone had walked into the room and whispered in my ear.*

Quickly I came out of my meditation, knowing full well that I needed a **Bible** *for my answer would be found there. Having been raised on the Bible in my childhood, I knew the passage would have something to do with Moses although I thought it would be about his birth or young years. It was not until I read the third chapter that I realized this was the story of Moses' confliction concerning leading his people, the people of Israel, out of Egypt. It was the story of his self-doubt, his wrestling with his own authority, his counsel from the Lord through the burning bush. I had learned that I gained deep insight when I interpreted the* **Bible** *in the Universal Language of Mind, and this was certainly no different, but by the time I read, "Tell them I AM sent you" it was very clear what my choice needed to be, could be, and would be.*

I now knew what I secretly hoped was indeed right. I could stand on my own. I could meet the challenges and make the changes. I could be and do as I imagined, and whatever I didn't know I could learn. I could bring enlightenment to a city.

Once the decision was made, all the energy was set into motion toward the fruition of this destiny. Within two weeks I had responsibly closed one chapter in my life and began a new one as director of the School of Metaphysics in Wichita.

This was the first time such a clear answer had come to me during meditation. To this time, the sense of clarity, calmness, joy, and peace were the answer to my prayers. Guidance usually came in a dream that night or sometimes in something that I heard, saw, or experienced during the day. This was my first experience of receiving a direct answer as a part of meditation. It came when I most sorely needed it. And I was so

very grateful for all the times I had made time for spiritual communion, for now when I needed help the most it was forthcoming.
And it has been ever since that day.

Since all greater creation has influence, power, and effect over all lesser creation it is important that you constantly strive to grow in your creative abilities. For my wife this meant physically moving to a city in another state. There she assumed the greatest challenge of her 22 years, putting her life in a new order, leaving the past behind and forging a new identity rooted in her constantly expanding sense of "who am I".

She was on her way to claiming that sense of greater creation within herself and her world. She discovered what is true for everyone who reaches this awareness, when you are constantly growing you are in a position to aid and benefit humanity in its soul growth and spiritual transformation. You desire to become an enlightened creator. The word enlightened means in light or with light or full of light. Therefore, it is important to understand the origin and essence of light. The origin of light and the connectedness with the Creator or higher intelligence is the true origin of the creative power within the Self.

1

What is meant by the term LIGHT?

Awareness.

2

What is I AM?

You are, I AM. I AM is you as an individual. It is your identity. I AM, is what you are and who you were when you were first created. I AM is the individualized unit of LIGHT that is you, the individual.

3

What is Mind?

Mind is a vehicle I AM uses to experience in order to gain permanent understandings.

4

What is Superconscious Mind?

The Superconscious Mind is the Source of life and Energy.

5

What is the Subconscious Mind?

The Subconscious Mind is the structure for enabling creative activity to take place.

6

What is the Conscious Mind?

The Conscious Mind is the creative aspect or forming structure of Mind.

7

*What is the purpose of I AM or the Self experiencing
in Mind?*

To gain permanent understanding of all Creation in
order to develop as a Creator.

8

Why is there more than one division of Mind?

Because the individual needs more than one type of
experience and more than one level of experience.

9

Why is one's individuality referred to as I AM?

As one develops in awareness and grows in consciousness one comes to understand that we exist in
the eternal now. The verb "was" is past tense
indicating the *past.* The words "will be" indicate
the *future.* I AM indicates the unique individual
that exists in the eternal now, *present.*

10

Why is I AM placed above Mind on the Mind chart?

I AM was created before and exists beyond vibratory creation beyond time and space.

Meditation and the Mind

The hour long meditation began first with a prayer,
followed by deep breathing and a specific chant.
In my prayer I asked to be close to the Creator.
Shortly after starting the meditation, my mind became very
still. Soon I felt a heaviness in my arms, as though they
weighed 100 pounds.
Then I reached a point where I felt myself moving within
my body. I saw a dark tunnel, and I heard a voice telling me
that I did have the capability to go to the inner levels.
When the meditation ended, it took me longer than usual to
bring my attention back to my physical body. I knew from that
point forward that I could reach this state of freedom from the
body whenever I desired.

It takes an investment to duplicate Kathryn's experience. Until you learn how to meditate you will spend most of your time in the Conscious Mind. The Conscious Mind is the division of mind associated with the brain, physical body, and five senses. The Conscious Mind will remain with you for only your lifespan on earth of 70 to 120 years or so.

The Subconscious Mind which is where the soul resides is permanent and will last as long as there is a single soul who needs to use it. All permanent learning which we may term understanding is stored in the individual's Subconscious Mind or soul. The temporary experiences you have this lifetime, the memories of experiences, and the sensory experiences will all be left behind at the end of this lifetime. What will remain is the you or the part of you that is eternal. The soul plus what you have gained this lifetime in the way of permanent understandings will remain as a part of you after this lifetime.

What determines if learning becomes understanding which then becomes permanent? For learning to be permanent, information must be reasoned with and found to be truth. Then the information, which has become knowledge through reasoning, must be applied in the life over and over until it becomes wisdom. Finally, the applied knowledge, called wisdom, must be taught to others so that the truth becomes a part of one's life. This is the process of producing understanding.

Meditation causes or creates an alignment of one's Conscious, Subconscious, and Superconscious Minds. The triangular effect in *Diagram 1* represents the scattering of attention that occurs as I AM, which is the individuality and identity that is you, moves through the Superconscious Mind, Subconscious Mind and Conscious Mind. I AM exists in the physical and Conscious Mind as the conscious ego. Everyone is an I AM. Everyone existing in the physical experience has a conscious ego.

The conscious ego is your motivator. The conscious ego is constantly motivating the Self to move forward by evolving, growing, changing, and transforming from a reasoning being to a higher level of being and existence.

The ultimate goal of each individual, each person, is to become compatible to and with our Creator. To do this we must evolve to become creators ourselves. A creator sees or perceives the physical existence as a temporary experience. Such a one improves the world for the benefit of not only Self but for all of mankind. This includes spiritual, mental, emotional, and physical improvement, growth, change, and development.

Since the natural tendency of energy and substance is to slow down and fragment as it moves from Superconscious, to Subconscious, to Conscious Mind it is incumbent upon each individual to counteract this natural effect of the scattering of energies and substance which causes the natural scattering of attention. The method or way to counteract this effect is to still the Conscious Mind.

The exercise of mental discipline and will can be employed to learn to control, focus, and direct the mind to a single point, object, or subject. Then the mind begins to become still. It was necessary to slow down the energies of Superconscious and Subconscious Minds in order that the five physical senses of sight, taste, touch, hearing, and smell would be able to detect the energies and substance in the physical world around us.

The physical senses experience physical things. We see a tree. We taste sweet or salty food. We smell a beautiful rose. We hear birds singing. We touch the earth on which we stand. All these are physical things. The Superconscious and Subconscious Minds are beyond the physical environment vibrating at a higher and more quickened rate than our dense, gross, physical objects and world.

Meditation carries you beyond the dense physicality of the material world and into the refined universe of the inner Subconscious and Superconscious Minds. One student describes his experience in this way:

When I meditated last week for 45 minutes, there was a point where I experienced a light emanating toward me, which is more unusual because I usually experience a light coming out of my forehead or all around me. The quality of this light seemed to be different, more holy or still in some way that at the moment I was unable to define. I received its energy into my core and yet somehow felt slightly distant from it, appearing in my mind's eye like the sun would in the sky on a clear summer day.

By stilling or quieting the Conscious Mind the conscious awareness or consciousness of the individual begins to move inward. Another way of stating this is: as the mind is still the consciousness of the individual aligns or identifies with and receives the higher vibratory rate and the higher energies of first Subconscious and then Superconscious Mind. The higher levels of Mind then become perceivable to the perceiver *(see Diagram 4 on next page)*.

A symbolizes the natural movement of energies from the beginning in Superconscious Mind all the way through Subconscious Mind out into the Conscious Mind and physical.

B represents one who has taken up the act of concentration. Such a one is practicing and doing a concentration exercise every day for at least 10 minutes and has also begun the process of meditation.

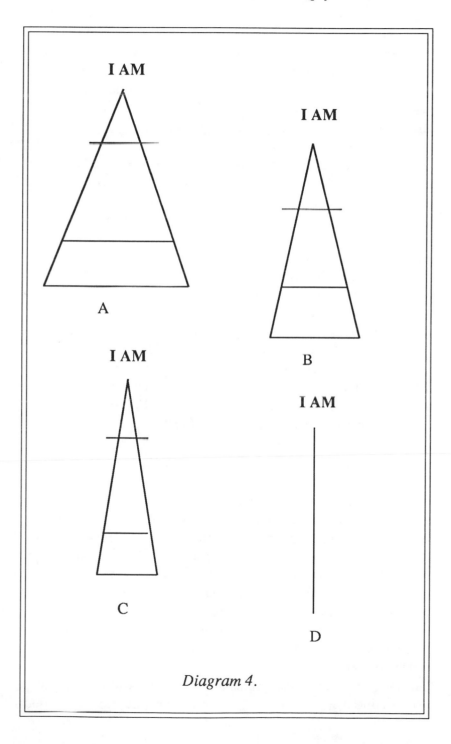

Diagram 4.

C indicates one who is becoming proficient with stilling the mind in meditation and who is applying this quiet, still mind in the daily life. Such a one has found peace within himself and is adding to his or her soul growth every day. This person also understands the value of giving what has been received and is therefore, teaching others about the Mind, Self and achieving their full potential as enlightened beings.

D is the one who has mastered Mind. Such a one has full control of his mind at anytime, in any place. Such a one can draw upon the higher knowledge of Subconscious and Superconscious Mind and therefore, has full access to Universal Truth. Such a one knows, I AM, for the conscious ego (small I AM) is fully aligned with the big EGO (I AM). Such a one has made a full commitment not only to his or her learning and growth but also to learning and growth of all mankind.

Such a one is a world teacher and world server – an individual whose main concern is the uplifting of mankind's consciousness and the quickening of its mental and spiritual evolution.

Such a one wields the Universal Laws for the benefit of Self and others. This one knows creation and Creator. He knows how creation works and functions. On a daily basis he is gaining greater insight and ability to be a Creator. He or she is one with the Creator and is gaining greater and greater compatibility with the Creator.

Such a one has become a helpmate, a helper, to the Creator in fulfilling the Creator's divine plan for the evolution of humanity and the world.

The meditator first begins to take control of the Conscious Mind by applying concentration, a focused mind, and a quiet or still mind in his life. As the student gains some mastery over the conscious, waking mind he is at the same time beginning to gain greater use, awareness and understanding of his Subconscious Mind. This is because as mental discipline is caused to occur in the Conscious Mind an alignment begins to occur with the Subconscious Mind. The Subconscious Mind only knows or identifies with forward motion, learning, and growth. The undisciplined mind identifies with re-action, limitation, habit, stagnancy, and the status quo.

The productive focused, disciplined, Conscious Mind also knows and identifies with learning, growth, and gaining the most value from each and every experience.

When the Conscious Mind is being productive by gaining the most from life experiences and adding to one's soul growth, then the Conscious Mind's goal and purpose aligns with the Subconscious Mind's goal and purpose .

The Subconscious Mind's goal is to be completely full of understandings. The Subconscious Mind's purpose is to store understanding.

The Conscious Mind has a goal also. The Conscious Mind's goal is to produce learning and growth for the whole Self. The Conscious Mind's purpose is to receive the fulfillment of its desires from the Subconscious Mind so that it may use these fulfilled desires to produce further learning and growth. This is called manifestation of your desires and learning to create from the process.

The Subconscious Mind will fulfill the desires of the Conscious Mind, if allowed to do so by the Conscious Mind for this is its duty. A limited, habitual, Conscious Mind has limits on its ability to receive and limits to its receptivity. Most everyone knows how difficult it is to give someone something if they do not want to receive it.

The Conscious Mind when habitual and undisciplined may be likened to the middle part of an hourglass. The middle part of an hourglass is very narrow therefore restricting the substance (usually sand) and energy that flows from the top. A habitual Conscious Mind restricts the movement of energy from Subconscious Mind to the Conscious Mind.

The Subconscious Mind does not restrict its giving. The Conscious Mind does, however, restrict its receiving by accepting limitations. The real Self is unlimited. The I AM is limitless because I AM exists above time and space. Space is a limit, as is time.

The Conscious Mind when caused to be productive works in harmony with the Subconscious Mind to produce rapid soul growth and spiritual development.

When the Conscious and Subconscious Mind are harmonized and working together for the benefit of the whole Self then these two great divisions of mind align with the third or other greater division of Mind which is the Superconscious Mind. At this point the individual experiences the divinity within Self, and a real and true connection with his or her Creator. Such a one is experiencing more and more what it is to be a spiritualized being.

To put it simply the Subconscious Mind of the individual has two jobs or duties. They are

1. *to store understandings*
2. *to fulfill the conscious mind's desires*

The Conscious Mind also has two jobs or duties. They are

1. *To glean experiences in order to*
2. *produce understandings from the experiences created in the physical existence*

In this way is the reasoning quality built within the Self so that the thinker may evolve to a higher level of consciousness.

My experience has shown me that the more you understand a process the better able you are to utilize that process. The more you understand about a car the better you are able to take care of that car. The more you understand about plants, the better garden you will grow. Therefore, this book about meditation will also instruct you in the understanding and use of the Mind. The Mind is the vehicle you will use in order to experience higher consciousness. Mind is the vehicle I AM uses to experience, learn, grow, and gain understandings. The Mind is what you have to work with in order to cause rapid soul growth and spiritual transformation.

When you still your conscious mind then and only then do you really know who you are as an I AM existing in the physical environment with a Conscious Mind. When you gain stillness of mind in both Conscious and Subconscious Minds; only then do you experience who you are as an I AM existing in Subconscious Mind.

When you gain stillness of mind in the Conscious, Subconscious, and Superconscious Minds, only then will you experience who you are as I AM existing in Superconscious Mind. At this point all three divisions of mind will be aligned and you will know your duty to help and aid all of humanity in quickening of its soul evolution. At this point of awareness you will know I AM for the three great divisions of Mind, Conscious, Subconscious and Superconscious will be aligned with I AM.

Different people use different nomenclature. You may have heard the term *Universal Mind.* You may ask, what is the difference between Universal Mind and Subconscious Mind?

Universal Mind is a term used to describe the quality of contraction of space, enhancement of communication and close connection that occurs in Subconscious Mind. In Subconscious Mind each of us has a mental hookup with everyone else, whether we use it or not. This mental or mind to mind connection is what makes telepathy possible.

When you have a telephone then you can phone a friend at a great distance. You can phone your parents. You can call your brothers or sisters who live in a distant city. If you decide to phone someone then you need to know their telephone number. The same is true of using the interconnectedness quality of Subconscious Mind to perform mental or mind to mind communication. Telepathy only works when you know how to use it and you learn to use it by first disciplining your conscious mind.

As you delve deeper and deeper into meditation you will more and more experience this interconnectedness of yourself with other people and, in fact, all of creation. You will first discover and later come to know how to connect with others on a deeper level. You will come to know how to use your mental telephone to mentally contact any other person regardless of whether they are near you or halfway around the earth.

One of Dr. Laurel Clark's meditation experiences illustrates this very well.

I had this experience in 1982, about three years after I had been meditating regularly every day.

I was in a very emotional state. I was planning to be married in a few weeks, and was having grave misgivings about it. I was beginning to realize that the character of the man I'd chosen to marry was not very good; I had been blinded to this when I decided to marry him. The problem was that all the plans were made and in place; we had sent out invitations to all of our friends and family. We had even started receiving gifts. Our relatives had purchased airplane tickets to come. We had reserved the place for the wedding and had put down deposits, and had ordered the cake and flowers. I had already looked for and found my wedding gown, and so forth.

So...at this late date it seemed impossible to do anything but go ahead with the plans.

*I needed to meditate and at first wanted to use my medita-
tion to answer the question, "should I go ahead with this
marriage or not?" Deep down inside I knew I did not want to
go ahead with it, but I was not objective and was being pulled
in every direction by my out-of-control ego and emotions.*

*I sat down to meditate and did everything I knew how to do
to try to still my mind. I was having difficulty keeping my mind
still. At first, I asked a question like, "What should I do?" and
received no answer. My mind kept running toward all of my
questions like, "What about my mother? How will I tell her?"
Suddenly I heard a clear voice (not my own) that said matter-
of-factly, "She'll adjust." Then I asked, "What about everyone
who has bought plane tickets?" Again, I heard that clear,
matter-of-fact voice, "They'll adjust." I asked in my thoughts,
"What about the people from whom we've reserved the
place?" The same calm, clear voice, "They'll adjust."*

*Every question I had, I received the same answer in the
same calm, clear, matter-of-fact objective voice. Gradually, my
own mind calmed down to the same state. I realized that I was
the one who had to adjust. I had a lot of ego invested in the
wedding and associated plans and a lot of attachment to the
idea of being married. I needed to adjust my attitude and draw
upon my own inner wisdom, because I hadn't faced the fact
that I'd made a poor choice in a marriage partner. The one-
time event of a wedding was a temporary thing, and although it
did mean I had to face some reactions from the people involved, those were temporary, too. Adjusting to change was the
important lesson for me, as well as adjusting to admit that I'd
made a mistake so that I could correct it before making an even
bigger one.*

*After this whole experience, my mind was clear and calm
and I was able to meditate. I realized that this experience was
not actually meditation, it was a communication with my guide.
She was the clear, calm Voice repeating, "they'll adjust." She
helped me be more objective so that I could be at peace with
my decision to call off the wedding.*

I learned several things from this experience. First, my

years of discipline doing concentration exercises and daily meditation paid off when I needed them. Although I was very emotional, I was able to hear the voice of my guide and know that it was she. Without the previous discipline, I probably would not have been still enough to hear anything other than my own undisciplined conscious thoughts. Second, I learned that meditation is not designed to make decisions for me. That's the job of the conscious mind, to choose, to decide. The reason I did not receive an answer to the question, "What should I do?" is because that's a question for the conscious mind to answer. The deeper question I had – "please help me to make a wise choice" – is what I received an answer to. My guide gave me another way to look at the situation. She did not make a decision for me; she helped me to view the situation from a more objective perspective without the emotional entanglements or attachments I had consciously.

A question and answer session with my guide was not in itself meditation, but it helped me to make the decision I needed to make so that I could clear my mind to meditate.

I learned something else: persistence pays off. When, at first, I did not receive the answer I sought, I did not give up. I stayed there in my meditation place, calmed my body and mind as best I knew how, and kept directing my attention toward what I wanted to receive. I received what I wanted and needed and also gave myself an experience I have been able to draw upon in the ensuing years to understand more completely how to use meditation.

Dr. Laurel's experience illustrates something else that becomes more apparent and therefore more readily usable with repeated meditations. Her meditation time enabled her to bring to the forefront of her conscious mind lines of thinking that had been unconscious. The trains of thought concerning what family and friends would think of her were unconscious until she settled her mind enough to allow them to surface. The degree to which they were unconscious is the degree to which she was controlled by them and about to make a serious life mistake. The urging "deep down inside" to alter the course of her life was the urging of her subconscious mind, her soul.

A confusion sometimes exists between the Subconscious Mind and the *unconscious* part of the brain. Some writers use the two terms interchangeably thereby showing their ignorance of Mind. The Subconscious Mind is not physical at all but is made of a more subtle, refined, essence or LIGHT that is vibrating at too high a rate to be perceivable by the five senses which only perceive gross physical matter. The unconscious is a function of the brain and the brain is a physical organ of the physical body.

When a person, particularly a child has an experience that is so frightening, sad, or overwhelming that the person is incapable of responding to it there is a tendency to partially wall-off the memory of that experience as a kind of protective device. However, this strategy is only partially successful because the walled-off memory continually bleeds into the present day experiences of the individual causing them to *re*-act at the strangest times and in the most irrational manner.

This strategy of closing a part of yourself off or of walling-off old memories only causes the person to live in those old memories and therefore to live in the past where the memories are. This means a person seems to exist in the present as they go through their day to day activities while mentally they are living in the past. This leads to terrible inefficiencies in life. It also creates re-actions, and irrational behavior. Because of this each person needs to meditate every day to learn that true security comes from within. Then there is no need to fear the old memories of which the person is only partially conscious or unconscious.

Dr. Pam Blosser's experience has much to give in illustrating how spiritual disciplines empower you to change because they create a new consciousness of self-revelation that becomes part of your thinking, awake or asleep, creative or meditative.

I have a nervous habit of picking at the dry skin around my fingernails. I knew this habit was based on a conscious thought from the past I had long since blocked out. Discovering the thought would help me break the habit.

On a visit to my family I set a goal to discover the thought that had eventually manifested into this nervous habit. One evening while in my former bedroom, I happened to pick up my high school annual and began thumbing through the pages. As

*I looked at the photographs and read what my friends had
written, in my mind I began to hear, "Never good enough.
Always second best. Never good enough, never good enough
nevergoodenough. Always second best."*

*In a flash of awareness I knew this was the thought which
had contributed to the nervous habit. It was a way of picking
on myself. In high school I was conscious of this thought.
Through the years it had gotten buried in my consciousness
where I wasn't aware of it anymore. However, it still existed as
it manifested in the nervous habit of physically picking on
myself.*

*As I pursued my mental disciplines I recognized that this
wasn't the only habitual, negative broken record that rattled
around in my head. There were others: ones of anger, hurt,
guilt, condemnation, and victimization. I became aware of how
I repeated parts of conversations in my head, things people
said that I had received as being hurtful and it generated anger
and hurt within me. I carried this static mental activity around
with me daily and into my meditations, making it difficult to still
my mind or achieve any deep states of silence. The broken
records had become mantras that kept my consciousness
trapped, like a rat in a cage, and I wanted to be set free from
the prison of negative thoughts. The practice of undivided
attention and concentration had brought this static once again
into my consciousness and sometimes I thought I would go
crazy hearing it all.*

*The process of learning to still my mind of this madness
began with a desire to be at peace. One way that I knew I
would gain peace was by knowing the truth. I knew that truth
would bring peace into my life. As the saying goes, "the truth
will set you free" and I believed the truth would set me free of
the misunderstandings I harbored that produced entrapment.*

*Breaking free of the broken records meant first of all,
replacing them with words and thoughts that were more
enlightening. Instead of repeating words of hurt, condemnation, guilt or blame over and over again I began to repeat
mantras that would open my mind to the benevolent reservoir*

of the universe. The first mantra was, "I want to know truth."
This thought opened my mind to receive more expanded ideas,
ones that I could depend on and would bring security.

Another mantra I began to use was. "Be Still and know
that I Am God." I would use this through the day and especially at times when I recognized my mind had been caught in
the rat race again. I would also use it before I started meditating. As I repeated the words, especially the words, "Be Still" I
would experience a vibrational wave flowing through me of
stillness where I would relax into a calmer state not only within
my physical body but also in my thinking.

There was an exercise I was given having the meditative
quality of communicating with Divinity by asking a question
and listening for the answer. This exercise was to ask, "What
would God have me do?" This was particularly productive
when I started to hear the rats in my head or when I began to
react to something. Because of my faith that God would
answer my prayers, I always received an answer that helped to
put that situation into perspective and calm me down.

Another practice was to observe my breathing throughout
the day. This is an ancient practice taught in the spiritual
disciplines of the world's religions, especially the East. It was
something I had begun years before with the practice of zazen
and now it had a greater purpose for me. Now I was watching
my breath to slow down my thinking, to cause it to be still and
in the moment so that I could gain the peace that I craved.

This process of freeing my mind from the rat cage was a
gradual one. It didn't happen overnight. It required determination and continual practice of different methods throughout
the day and in meditation.

With continued desire, determination, and practice my
meditations have become stiller and stiller, deeper and deeper.
Now deep meditations are just as important to me each day as
eating, or sleeping. I feel my day is incomplete if I have to cut
my meditations short before I reach a deep state.

The moments of anxiety are farther apart and more short-
lived. I am less entrapped in them. And my consciousness is

expanding to include not only the experiencer but also the
observer and learner of the experience. I am breaking free of
the temporary ego states of pleasure and pain and getting
closer and closer to my true nature of joy.

Sometimes people do not have the knowledge, experience, reasoning, or wisdom to deal with, come to terms with, and understand these experiences they have stored unconsciously in the brain as misunderstandings. These unconscious misunderstandings, fears, doubts, guilts, and limitations intrude on one's outer life. They affect and limit everything that person does. It becomes a part of his personality.

However, the personality is dropped off or left behind each lifetime with death and disintegration of the physical body. In this way you start off each lifetime with a clean slate and with no negativity or limitations. You bring with you each lifetime your accumulated understandings that wait to be brought forth by the disciplined, meditative thinker.

Your first step in learning to meditate is to learn to focus and direct your attention which is called concentration. This developed ability to concentrate will then be used to still your mind in meditation.

Every day choose an object on which to concentrate. You may choose a doorknob, a dot on the wall, or the tip of your index finger which works very well. Remember, do not think while concentrating. If thoughts arise allow them to pass through your consciousness giving them no attention. Gradually or quickly your mind will become disciplined and come under the control of you, the thinker. Then you are ready for meditation.

1

What does it mean to meet God face to face in meditation?

The student should have as their ideal to do much more than see or meet God face to face. Think about it. Would you want to just look at your physical father or mother face to face or would you want to embrace your mother and father? Would you like to go beyond embracing, coming to know your mother and father and eventually becoming compatible with them? Of course you would. In the same manner it is important to strive and to hold the image of expanding your consciousness to enter into the Mind of God. Your goal is to know God and to realize God and to expand your consciousness to fill all of creation as God's consciousness does.

2

It's easy to see God in the things around me and outside of myself—but I have difficulty in seeing God as being within. How do I change this?

Stop seeing yourself as separate and apart from creation. Rather recognize you are *a part* of creation. In this way you come to be one with others, you come to be one with everything in creation while at the same time adding to your own identity and understanding of your unique individuality as an offspring of the Creator.

3

*Ever since about two months after I started medi-
tating, when I close my eyes and turn them upward,
after a few minutes I see this purple spot which is a
little darker than pastel purple. It appears to be a
few inches out in front of me, just a little above the
third eye area. I have never known what it is, but I
know when I see it, I'm "there". What is this
purple area I see ?*

It is a doorway into the inner levels of Mind. It may
be used as such. I suggest you first practice concentration until you can control your thoughts and
still your mind. In this way you will have control in
the inner levels of mind when you enter there. The
next step beyond this is to learn to expand your
consciousness to include all levels of mind and all
parts of creation.

4

*Sometimes after meditation I am really tired and I
want to sleep. This happens even when I have been
awake and alert through the whole meditation.*

True meditation does not leave you tired. On the
contrary, it invigorates you. Meditation does however, leave you feeling relaxed. In true meditation
the body is very relaxed. The muscles relax more
than at any other time, maintaining just enough
tension to hold the back, neck, and head upright. If
you are tired after meditation it is because you are
not relaxed during meditation and are therefore, not
really getting your attention off your physical body.

5

Why do I fall asleep sometimes during meditation? This happens even when my posture is straight. What are some things I can do to stay awake during meditation?

The reason you fall asleep in meditation is that you need to develop a strong will and will power. Will power is mental not physical. At night when you go to sleep the Conscious Mind shuts down and the attention shifts to Subconscious Mind. Therefore, you have developed a habit of going to sleep when your attention moves or shifts from Conscious to Subconscious Mind. Learn to cause yourself to go to sleep rather than falling asleep when you go to bed at night. In meditation we desire for the attention to leave the Conscious Mind and move first into Subconscious Mind and then Superconscious Mind. You need to use your will to overcome this habit of losing consciousness when entering the Subconscious Mind. This will require practice, time and effort. Practice exerting your discipline, will, and concentration more in your waking life, throughout the day.

First you must learn to still your mind and concentrate and then you can learn to expand your consciousness into the higher levels of mind.

6

How do I integrate expectant listening and observation stages into meditation?

First learn to still your mind and remove your attention from your body during meditation. Learn to still your mind at anytime during your day. Give your undivided attention to everything you do. Learn to receive through all five senses without any walls of separation or protection around yourself. Be ready to receive at all times in meditation.

7

How can I present a prayer, question or thanksgiving, in order to have a clear meditation?

You must first learn to form a clear mental image of your prayer or petition. If you desire to understand love then formulate a picture of love. If you desire peace then ask for peace and image peace. The mind works from mental images. Then release this picture or mental image to Subconscious Mind.

In order to have a clear meditation be open, receptive, and surrendering in your attitude to the higher consciousness.

8

What are some examples of how to formulate and ask specific questions for soul growth during meditation?

Focus in your prayer or petition on qualities of greatness and enlightenment such as love, peace, joy, bliss, and expanded wisdom and understanding.

9

What is the highest meditation experience?

Receiving from the Divine.

10

How can I expand my consciousness and receive at the same time?

Since the Divine is in all creation you must first image receiving from the Divine.

Sacred Time

Meditation is the time you make to image and receive from the Divine.

When Melanie, a middle-aged mother of two first began meditating, she realized a heightened sense of love that she had never before known. The experience during this meditation session became the one by which she measured all future efforts for it was an experience she wanted to repeat, again and again.

> *I started practicing meditation a few weeks after entering the School of Metaphysics. Meditation was a new concept to me. I had never done anything like this and really did not know what to expect. I had been practicing for two or three weeks when one day I came home from work on a day when every-thing seemed to go wrong. As I prepared myself for meditation I was in a state of mind where I really needed guidance. Even more than that, I needed love. I felt very alone and in despair. I prepared my petition. All I wanted was to know that I was loved and that God was there for me.*
>
> *Immediately upon completion of expanding my light and opening myself to the universe I felt love pour into my being. I perceived a cone of light starting from a point beyond the ceiling of my room and extending over my physical body. It appeared pink in color and was very warm and embracing. I sat there in that light and let the love of God pour into me, tears rolled from my eyes and I knew that I was loved.*

Sometimes as in this case the meditator will experience a great feeling or perception of joy, love, light or expansion of consciousness going far beyond anything they have previously experienced and they receive this clear and higher perception of reality soon after learning to meditate. When this occurs it is a clear statement from the inner Subconscious and Superconscious Minds of the great possibilities and potentialities that the person may attain over time in meditation and the correctness of what she is doing. The meditator may not be able to re-create this experience immediately but has been given a taste of what can be made a part of Self permanently by persisting in their meditative attempts. By getting a higher perception of reality and a more expansive perception of what one can become the desire is increased immensely to have and make a part of oneself that higher state of consciousness.

God did create the universe and everyone in it as an act of love. So naturally, when this mother formed her desire to know – her petition, around the thought of knowing God – she received an experience of love. In God, love is complete. God's love is constantly surrounding us and available. Meditation is the receiving of the Creator. Each person needs to raise their consciousness and open themselves completely to receive this higher love. The result is truly life-transforming, as the following College of Metaphysics student, Shannon, learned:

> *I experienced my greatest meditation in November 1996 at a Spiritual Initiation Session. The theme presented that weekend caused me to think about what the Creator means to me. I discovered the answer when I meditated before the closing circle (of love). The excitement boiled through me!*
>
> *I found* **Love** *inside myself, deep down under, behind the protective walls where I so often hide; hiding from the Creator. I found openness and honesty. I found security within myself. I touched my Soul and fulfilled a desire to learn if I had any Love inside to share with others as well as myself.*
>
> *How freeing it is to know if I'm ever in doubt, I can meditate and find the answer. It's there.*

It is each person's duty to touch their soul this lifetime and each lifetime. Following this it is each person's duty to come to know who they are as a soul. The circle of love Shannon cites is an experience of love given and received by the students of the School of Metaphysics at the end of each class. Students are taught how to touch their own soul. They learn how to cause their inner light and love to grow enabling them to share these with others. As they understand the nature of their own light and love they can expand them to create a circle of love which empowers them to touch other souls realizing their oneness with others.

Meditation enhances this learning, and encourages the realization of uniting with the Creator.

True security comes from the inner Self, the soul. Physical possessions provide a type of physical, temporary security of having your needs provided for. They are important. True permanent, lasting, universal security comes from the soul and is built when the Conscious Mind Self is in alignment with and serving the Subconscious Mind Self or soul.

No one should feel the need to hide behind protective walls for those walls are, in fact, your prison that keep you from learning and experiencing all the goodness, learning, and joy of the world. This is why you need inner security, so you don't need the walls of so-called protection that actually repel other people and keep you separate and alone. As Shannon's inner walls between herself and her God vanished, so did the distance diminish between herself, her friends and family and acquaintances.

Answers are always available in meditation when you still your mind and listen to the inner Self. As you first begin meditating, listening for the answer to your question or prayer with your mind or mental ear has top priority. As your meditation deepens from regular practice your consciousness expands. You learn to look forward to the experience of peace, Love, LIGHT, and unity and interconnectedness even more. For the expansion of consciousness is the answer to your prayers.

An author and a spiritual teacher for two decades, Dr. Laurel Clark remembers one of her most meaningful meditations in this way:

The first Spiritual Initiation Session I conducted included a series of meditations over a period of two days. All of the meditations were done with a small group of people; some were outside on a stone porch overlooking the woods and some were inside in a warm, inviting living room. The setting was serene, peaceful, and quiet: no telephones, and the opportunity to concentrate completely on inward reflection.

As the weekend progressed, I was aware of becoming more and more still, more and more centered, more and more peaceful.

The highlight was a meditation in the morning, shortly after sunrise. We had done some gentle stretching and hatha yoga exercises, outside on the grass, including a series of

*movements called The Sun Salutation. Then we went for a walk
in the brisk morning air (it was the beginning of March, chilly
and sunny). We walked down a hill through the woods, across
a field, and back up through the woods, hearing the crunch of
leaves underfoot, smelling the fresh air, feeling refreshed and
energized. We settled down to meditate on the big stone porch.
The air was cool, the sun was warm, the birds were softly
chirping. My body was relaxed and invigorated. I prepared for
meditation by breathing deeply, then we chanted AUM. I felt
and heard the sound reverberating, and in combination with
the other people meditating it was as if the sounds produced
overtones. My attention was drawn more and more inward as
we chanted.*

*Then the meditation. My mind was still, and I could not
feel my physical body at all. I felt as if I was wrapped in a
warm embrace of light. The light was within me and all around
me. I experienced a tremendous and powerful love, soothing,
strong, warm, and secure. I "felt" myself smiling, although my
mouth didn't move, my whole being was uplifted and happy. I
don't know how long I stayed in this state of bliss. It seemed
like I could stay there forever. When I did finally bring my
attention back to my body and physical surroundings, I didn't
want to move.*

*I sat there for a long time, not moving my physical body,
looking at the beautiful scene before my eyes: the woods, wisps
of fog and mist nestled in the trees, the sunlight filtering
through the tree branches. It looked incredibly beautiful. I felt
very connected with the other people who were meditating, as if
I were in love with them and everything else around me. I was
calm and peaceful inwardly along with a sense of exuberance,
joy, and vitality.*

As I noted at the beginning of this chapter, the Spiritual Initiation
Sessions are held on the College of Metaphysics campus which is over
1500 acres located in the beautiful Ozark Mountains of Southern Missouri. During these weekend retreats participants are led through stages
of Self awareness, Self discovery, and Self understanding by the spiritual

leaders who have achieved the Doctorate of Metaphysics from the School of Metaphysics and the College of Metaphysics.

AUM is a chant used in meditation and is akin to OM, the sound of Creation revered in several Eastern religious practices. AUM also represents the trinity as given in the <u>Bible</u> of *Father* (Superconscious Mind), *Son* (the aggressive Conscious Mind striving to know the whole Self), and the *Holy Spirit* (the whole Mind). *Holy* and the word *whole* come from the same root word or source.

When during meditation you achieve a state where you no longer feel your physical body, you have moved your attention within and away from your physical attachments and engrossment. The mind is then free to soar to great heights of spiritual awareness. The light is awareness, the Light of the Creator is always around us. It is up to each individual to learn to receive that Light. Meditation is a receptive act. When the attention goes within to the inner levels of Mind you are much closer to your Creator and your walls of self-imposed protection are down so you are able to receive the Light and love of the Eternal, Supreme which clearly exists in Superconscious Mind.

Bliss is that state of communion with the Creator. It is the alignment of Subconscious and Conscious Minds and their attunement with Superconscious Mind. It seemed to Dr. Laurel that she could stay there forever because she achieved a state of consciousness beyond time and space. She achieved Superconscious awareness.

Everything in Creation is beautiful when seen through the perception of the Superconscious Mind. There is a full connection and unity in Mind. The deeper or higher you go into Mind the less separation you experience, the less physical time and space you experience.

For deep in Mind you are timeless, eternal, and everywhere.

Chapter Two

The Conscious Mind

My second experience with a type of meditation was in the autumn, or fall as we always called it. It was a pleasant fall day and I was walking in the woods. I came upon a ditch that was filled with leaves that had fallen off the trees in the woods. The leaves were at least three foot deep. I laid down in the leaves on my back so I could look up at the clear, blue sky.

The leaves made the softest bed I had ever lain on. I sank down in them. I noticed a few fleecy, white, clouds in the sky. My mind was still and I was at peace. In fact, it was the most peaceful feeling I had ever experienced. Once again I was among the trees.

I laid there for quite some time, silently experiencing the peace and tranquility.

Years later I was in college. I was enrolled in a speech class. The teacher mentioned there was a program available that anyone could attend that was experimental and that might give people more confidence giving speeches. I decided to go.

When I arrived the instructor had everyone lie down on their backs on the carpeted floor. Then he instructed us to visualize ourselves going to the most relaxed place we had ever been. I remembered the leaves I had laid in at my father's woods. After we had completely relaxed while visualizing ourselves being in this relaxed place he then had us visualize ourselves giving a speech while still maintaining this relaxation. Thus, we visualized ourselves giving a speech and being relaxed doing it.

When we finished the relaxation I got up off the floor and went outside. I opened the big, tall doors of the hundred-year-old, red brick building and saw the rain coming down. There was water on the sidewalks and on the grass of the beautiful college campus and it was wonderful. I felt alive. I felt more alive than anytime I could remember. I felt so alive that I took my shoes and socks off and ran over one quarter of a mile to the building where I lived. I was free and the experience was exhilarating as I ran barefoot through the puddles of water on this warm fall day.

The calmness of body and concentrated, visualizing mind enabled me to focus my thoughts and still my mind. Thus, my mind became free of its entrapment to the physical body. There was an alignment of the inner and outer minds. This produced the freedom, exhilaration, and bliss I experienced.

The Conscious Mind is one of three divisions of Mind; the other two being the Subconscious Mind and the Superconscious Mind. The Conscious Mind is the division of Mind that works directly with the brain and the five senses. The brain is an organ of the physical body that the conscious mind utilizes in order to reason in the physical existence. The brain is equipped with a storage mechanism called memory in order that events from the past can be recalled to aid in effectively responding in the present.

The Conscious Mind also has a physical structure with which to interact in the now. These devices are the five senses. The five senses are constantly receiving impressions from the physical environment. Each operates at a different vibratory wavelength. Together the five senses provide the individual with a set of experiences that can be responded to.

In order to move forward in life the thinker needs a vehicle for creating and preparing for the future. The image maker or directed imagination provides the key. The physical structure associated with the imaging capability that is located in the brain is the pituitary gland. The faculty of imagination and the gland of perception, the pituitary, make possible the outpouring of imagination that drives people to create and build a better life, a better world, and a greater tomorrow.

Since the five senses together perceive only a small portion of the total experience of creation around us it is of utmost importance that each person learn to cultivate the higher faculties of the mind. In this way they can come to know all of creation and all its vibration, movement, and manifestation.

The great and secret key to all of creation is mental images or mental pictures. The imagination relies on mental images or mental pictures. Memory recall is the process of drawing forth mental images or pictures from the brain in order to review them. Full attention is the ability to place your mental attention on one place in order to fully receive the mental images emanating from that person, place or object. The mind is keyed to mental images. At night, dreams are conveyed as a type of communication from the Subconscious to the Conscious Mind in the form of mental images.

Communication from one person to another verbally requires that the person speaking or sending the message choose words that accurately portray the message held as an image in the speaker's mind. The receiver or listener must also receive the complete verbal communication in order to erect a reasonable facsimile in their mind's eye of the mental image the speaker desired to communicate.

The power of the Conscious Mind is the faculty of reasoning. Reasoning is the factor that sets man the thinker, whether male or female, apart from the animals. Animals possess memory. Animals also possess the capability for attention. It is the faculty of imagination that animals have not developed. All three qualities – memory-past, attention-present, and imagination-future – are necessary for reasoning to occur. In humans the brain is enlarged and the frontal part of the brain cavity exists to enable reasoning to occur as directed by the Conscious Mind.

All great inventions were first created in the mind's eye or imagination of the inventor before being brought into physical manifestations. Every person who has ever made a great contribution to the world for the betterment and uplifting of mankind has first imaged their desire daily for months and years until the physical environment began to match what had been imagined. Activity, action, and continual forward motion toward the imaged ideal eventually produced the creative change in the physical environment for Self and others which is called creation.

The Conscious Mind is that part of Mind that each of us uses consciously every day. It is the division of Mind we use in conjunction with the five senses of touch, taste, smell, sight, and hearing. It is the part of Mind that we use to reason with each day to whatever degree each individual is capable of reasoning. The brain is a physical organ that is used by the Conscious Mind. Mental images called memories are stored in the brain. New mental images can be added to these through the use of attention and imagination. Attention receives current mental images from the environment while imagination creates new images of the future or of the possible future.

The Conscious Mind, when disciplined, directs the energies of the brain. When the Conscious Mind is undisciplined the brain is predominant over the Conscious Mind. The brain is the animal part of the thinking apparatus. Animals have brains. Reptiles have brains. Fish have brains. Mammals have brains. As we move up the evolutionary ladder the animal brain becomes more highly developed. The human brain is so highly developed it can house, hold, contain, develop, and entrap a soul in the Conscious Mind. The soul then residing in the Conscious Mind uses the brain and the physical body for the length of that body's lifetime.

The Conscious Mind must be created new each lifetime. The physical brain also must be created anew each lifetime. The physical brain is created in the mother's womb as part of the physical body. It is a product of the genetics of the two parents. The Conscious Mind, however, is built up by the soul inhabiting the physical body particularly in childhood. For the first seven years of life the Conscious Mind is a product of the environment that the child grows up in. This is the time in which the personality is formed. This is the time in which the foundation of learning is created in the brain of the child that will serve as the parameter for what the individual is to achieve for that lifetime. The most important influence and factor in the early development of the Conscious Mind are the father and mother. This is why it is vitally important for the parents, especially the mother to be at home and raise the child instead of a day care or baby sitter raising the child.

Do the father and mother love the child? Do they give the child lots of loving attention? Are they positive in giving the child lots of smiles and encouragement? These are some of the most important factors in a child's early development. On the other hand, do they often ignore the child, refuse to discipline the child and give little love? Parents are much more than role models. The child who is taught to discipline the Self early in life will find that when he is ready for Self discipline and mental discipline of Self that the discipline that is required for meditation will come much easier for there is already a foundation of discipline built within Self.

The brain is a vehicle or tool the conscious mind uses to carry out its duty to the subconscious mind and to the whole Self. The brain being the animal part of Self will attempt to assert control over the conscious mind and the whole Self. One who is mentally undisciplined has an animal brain that is in control of the Self. The animal and animal brain operates from a fight or flight thought process. This limits his options. A thinker, a person who is using reasoning with a disciplined, concentrated, conscious mind knows he has more options. He can harmonize with the Universal Laws and create what is necessary in the life. A cow given enough grain will eat herself to death. A human, a thinker, knows she needs to balance the physical with the mental and spiritual. Instead of waiting for the environment to dictate whether one will flee or fight, the reasoner creates the situations and circumstances desired in the life. Such a one does not allow the physical environment to restrict the Self.

Before a child is born, while still in the womb he begins to receive impressions from those in the environment. The child also receives thoughts and emotions from those in the environment. The child begins to mimic these thoughts, emotions, and impressions. After the birth of the child has occurred this process of receiving ideas and thoughts from those in the environment continues. The child begins to assimilate these vibrations and begins to act like the parents.

A newborn is hungry and so he cries. In response, the mother of the baby breastfeeds him. The child stores this information in the brain automatically. The child's brain also registers the love, warmth, safety, and security he receives from the mother who is breastfeeding him.

The child has a wet diaper and cries. The mother changes the diaper and lovingly holds the child. This also the child registers and begins to assimilate. This process of eliciting responses and gathering experiences continues as the child grows to the age of seven. During the first seven years of life the child's learning may be likened to the way a sponge soaks up water. As a sponge soaks up water within itself so also does a child soak up experiences, information, thoughts, and emotions into her body and brain.

By the age of seven the child has accumulated enough information, memories, and mental images into the brain to initiate the process of reasoning. The period of the most rapid receiving of learning is over. Reasoning must progress from infancy to childhood through adolescence and into adulthood. Around the age of 14 the child has accumulated enough information, experience, and knowledge to use the stage of learning called adolescence of reasoning.

This is where mankind exists today, in its present level of development; adolescence of reasoning. This is one reason why there is so much conflict in the world. In order to enter into a true age of peace mankind must move forward and evolve into the stage called adulthood of reasoning.

True adults are willing to still their mind and listen to one another. True adults are secure and confident enough within themselves that they are able to ask questions and listen which is the true hallmark of communication.

An animal operates from the fight or flight re-action. The thinker, one who is in the stage of learning called adulthood of reasoning asks questions and listens and then formulates responses based upon accurate knowledge.

Meditation is a process of asking questions and listening for the answer to your prayer, petition, or question. Most people, having an undisciplined mind do not really know how to listen. When you have a conversation with them they are so busy thinking of their next question that they don't hear your answer to their first question.

In order to be able to hear the answer to a question you must first still your mind. To be able to receive you must have a still mind. Have you ever seen a pool of water or a pond on a day where there is little or no wind? If so, you noticed that there were no waves on the water. When you throw a rock in a still pool of water or pond you will notice it makes a ripple or waves proceeding out from the point where the rock hit the water until the waves reach out to the farthest reaches of the pond.

The mind may be likened to this pond of water. The wind may be likened to the thoughts of the individual. A rock may represent outside influences that you allow to influence or control your peace of mind.

On a windy day the surface of the water will already have waves due to the action of the wind. Therefore, when you throw a rock into this choppy, wavy, water, the waves created from the rock are immediately overpowered by the waves from the wind.

In a similar manner when the wind of your thoughts is blowing so strongly across the water of your mind then any rock-thoughts or communication you receive from another person is immediately overpowered and destroyed by your own undisciplined thoughts. The result is you don't really understand what the person just said.

If the water of your mind is still then when you receive a thought from another your consciousness is able to perceive the waves created in your consciousness by the action of receiving another's thoughts. Therefore, you understand the thoughts of another and your mind is free to expand and grow from the interaction.

An undisciplined mind cannot grow. A closed mind cannot grow. A still, quiet, and disciplined mind can expand into infinity.

It is truly amazing but most people are a product solely of their upbringing. Whatever limitations people have taught them as children is what they accept. Fortunately, for the progression of mankind, there are a few individuals who do not accept the limitations of their environment and their upbringing. Fortunately also, a few parents teach their children to go beyond all limitations and learn from every situation. Those few, between one and ten percent cause 99% to 100% of the growth and motion of humanity through the arts, sciences, religion, technology, and so on.

Meditation enables you the individual, to break out of whatever limitation you may have accepted. Each person comes into this lifetime with a certain set of understandings. Each person's total collection of understandings is different from everyone else's. Some people have more permanent understandings stored in their subconscious mind than others. These people are the true enlightened leaders of society and civilization. When civilization is led by the enlightened then humanity progresses. When it is led by the unenlightened the society decays. Enlightenment is not an all or nothing situation. Enlightenment occurs in stages. The highest level of enlightenment is called Christ Consciousness, Buddha Consciousness, God Consciousness or God Realized, depending on what country, time period, and society you exist in.

Meditation is an exact science in that it will work for anyone who is willing to discipline the mind and body and be consistent in practicing on a regular daily basis. Meditation always involves stilling the conscious mind and directing the attention inward first to the subconscious mind and then to the superconscious mind. At first the meditator notices restlessness within the mind and body. Later, with persistence, the body reacts less and less to the discipline of sitting still in one position for 15 minutes, 30 minutes, or longer.

A financial planner, mentally in the rush of metropolitan life, Cheryl found the first rewards of meditation were profound in their simplicity.

I have felt the stillness and quiet of my mind. The slowing of
the bodily functions and to know stillness and peace.

In order to meditate successfully the meditator must learn to quiet and then still the mind. The body needs to slow down and relax so you can remove your attention from the physical body. Obviously, since you want to move your attention deep into Mind to know yourself, you must learn to remove your attention from your physical body.

The peace that Cheryl experienced was a sure sign she is receiving benefits from meditation. The conscious mind when willed by the person over time begins to slow down and to become more quiet. By this I mean that the incessant progression of thoughts such as worries, guilts, fears, and desires arise in the conscious mind less and less. This is due to the meditator refusing to give attention to the thoughts and instead placing the attention on listening for the answer to his or her prayer, question, or petition posed at the beginning of meditation.

Because most people have spent many years trying to do many tasks at one time and causing their mind to race in an effort to "keep up" or to get more things done faster it requires some effort to re-train the conscious mind to the idea of the need and benefits of slowing and stilling the thoughts in the conscious mind. Have you ever noticed that hurrying slows you down. Hurried people are terribly inefficient. The one who practices meditation soon discovers that stilling the mind and learning to focus the attention is the easiest and most efficient way to use the mind. It is also the way to get the most done in a minute, an hour, a day, a week, a month, a year, and a lifetime. All the great thinkers throughout history have learned to focus their minds in order to accomplish the tremendous feats they achieved. The great spiritual leaders were, not only people of tremendous vision, but also men and women of incredible focus and concentration.

When the conscious mind is stilled and thoughts stop arising in the conscious mind only then is the individual able to receive instruction, knowledge, and wisdom from the subconscious mind. Think about this.

If you are talking to another person and you ask them a question. If while that other person is answering your question you are busy thinking up the next question then there is no way that you can hear the other person's response. At best you will only hear part of that response because part of your attention will be upon thinking of the next question. In other words your attention is divided or split between two or more areas.

While meditating the one meditating needs to give undivided attention to listening for the answer to your prayer or question. If your petition is stated thusly, "Dear God, I desire to learn about love," then you need to listen intently with undivided attention, waiting with a still mind for the answer to your question or petition.

When you are out in nature you will need to give it your whole attention if you want to experience nature fully. What good does it do you to spend time in nature only to be thinking of your problems and stresses at work or the argument you had with a loved one 6 months ago or your fear of asking for a raise at work or of driving to a new city? In order to gain the most from each experience you must be fully in the now. Your attention must be where you are or where you have chosen to be. In this case, meditation.

You exist in the present so cause your attention to be fully in the present. As you practice concentration you become a deeper thinker. A good way to begin the practice of concentration is to focus your attention on the second hand of a clock for 5 minutes. Gradually increase this to 10 minutes. If your attention wanders then bring it back to the second hand over and over until your attention has been trained to stay where you want it anytime for as long as you choose to keep it there.

Most people fail to use the understandings they have earned in past lives due to the fact that they do not discipline their conscious mind. By meditating every day you will find that the permanent understanding that you have earned and stored from past lifetimes begins to come to the forefront of your consciousness. Remember, a disciplined mind is a receptive mind. A disciplined mind is receptive and, therefore, able to receive understandings stored in the individual's subconscious mind. This makes that person a formidable force in causing world change, growth, and expansion of consciousness.

A person who is satisfied with accepting only what others or someone has put into them either consciously or unconsciously in the way of

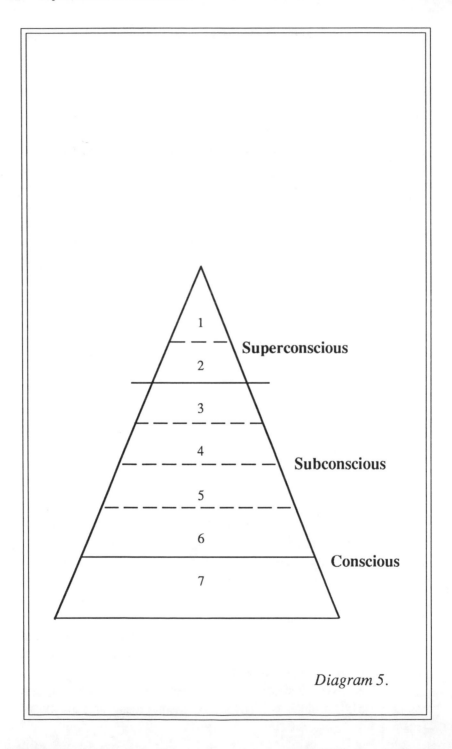

Diagram 5.

limitations and limited information and experiences will never know who they are and what is the real self. Such people will always be living someone else's thoughts, someone else's ideas about life and someone else's limitations.

The Conscious Mind is the only one of the three divisions of Mind that is not further divided into levels (see *Diagram 5* on the previous page). This is because originally envisioned and created in the seventh level of Mind, the physical existence, was meant to be a place where entities, that is, souls, could learn through observation. The seventh level of Mind was designed so that souls could learn through receptivity rather than activity. Since the time of entrapment, the people of humanity, who are actually individual souls incarned and entrapped in a physical body, have needed to learn through action. While incarned in a physical body, the soul that is you learns through activity and action. The physical or 7th level of Mind is the part of Mind that works with and is dependent upon the five senses. When you smell the odor of a kind of food you have eaten before and enjoyed, you remember the flavor and odor and your mouth begins to water or salivate in preparation for the food. So memory in the conscious mind is intimately connected with and used in conjunction with the five senses.

After you learn to drive a car you can get in the car and remember how to start the car and drive it. The same is true for dribbling a basketball or using an ax to chop wood or painting with a brush or whipping cream with a whisk. You, the thinker, build your conscious mind from the time you were born. When the newborn baby cries it hears the sound with its auditory sense and gains a new bit of information. When the baby is fed or the diaper is changed the baby receives more information. In this way the conscious mind is built as information, experience, and knowledge is achieved.

The brain continues to gather information and experience to be stored as memory. By the time the child is 14 years old the attention of most children has been so drawn outward away from the inner self into the physical through sensory experience that the subconscious mind, the abode of one's soul, has been completely forgotten or covered by the conscious mind. This is unfortunate as the subconscious mind holds millennia of knowledge and wisdom just waiting to be utilized by the receptive and Self aware individual. The child can be trained from birth to use the physical body, brain, and five senses while still retaining the ability to draw on and to have awareness in Subconscious Mind.

The first step in teaching a child to learn to use his mind to the fullest is to constantly give him attention, love, and teaching. Teaching to the young child is giving him the information about his environment so he can store the information in his brain.

Walk around the kitchen while holding the child. Point to a cup and say the word "cup". Point to a spoon and say the word "spoon" aloud to the child. This gives the child a way to build singular attention while at the same time learning to identify objects in her environment.

Put one red dot on the wall. Point to the red dot and say the word "one". Then put two red dots on the wall and say to the child the word "two". Then do this with three dots, four dots, and so on in order that the child learns the concept of numbers and quantity while building the faculty of attention.

As the ability to give attention grows, show the child how to look at the second hand of a clock as it makes one revolution. This is the beginning of concentration.

Take the child with you to the woods where it is quiet so he may experience the quietness of a still mind. Make sure that every day the child has a time when he is in a quiet environment.

A noisy environment produces in the child a noisy mind with scattered attention. What we desire is a quiet and still mind for meditation.

By now the child may have learned to sit still for a short time. That is the beginning of meditation.

Certain children are born as child prodigies and geniuses. The understanding of music, art, science, and spiritual development has already been made a part of that individual's subconscious mind, their permanent Self, before they were born. This lifetime they are able naturally or have been taught by their parents how to draw out this permanent knowledge called understandings.

Ten, 20, 30, 40, 50, 60, or even 70 years in a lifetime is not by itself enough physical time to allow for some of the magnificent inventions and creations bestowed upon humanity by certain geniuses.

Albert Einstein developed his famous Theory of Relativity after having a dream about riding a beam of light. Nikola Tesla, who far surpassed Thomas Edison as a genius in the field of electricity, invented the alternating current system of electricity which is used worldwide today and in the house or apartment you live in. While Thomas Edison was promoting a direct current system of electricity transfer which was very inefficient, Nikola Tesla gained his insight only after months of pondering over how to build an alternating current electric system and being told by his college professors it could never be done. One day after pondering on this problem for many hours he went for a walk in the local park. It was at this time while his thoughts were stilled and his mind was quiet, peaceful, and in a receptive state that the solution came to him as he stood gazing at the beautiful sunset not even thinking about the problem he was working on solving.

You see his conscious mind had been prepared and was receptive because Tesla had learned everything he could about electricity. All knowledge, currently available on earth concerning this subject he had mastered. At the time of gazing at the setting sun his mind had entered a condition of expectant receptivity which enabled his conscious mind to receive the higher knowledge, the answer or solution to his question in a flash of brilliance. Shortly thereafter, Tesla created the alternating current electric motor and generator which enhances our lives today. Meditation is your tool for drawing on the higher knowledge of the inner Mind.

John is a recent high school graduate who has been studying metaphysics for almost two years. He is pursuing full-time study at the College of Metaphysics, knowing what he learns here will aid him to identify his soul's purpose for this lifetime and will then help him fulfill that purpose with the choices that shape the course of his unfolding adult life. His meditations are deepening, and the accompanying realizations he is making are to be devoutly desired at any age.

The most profound meditation I have ever had was focused around the topic "inspiration." I knew that sometimes I was inspired to act and sometimes I wasn't. I knew how it felt to be inspired, the emotion and the power over yourself and your destiny. That is exactly what I imagine superconscious awareness to be, except all the time. I meditated on that for about twenty minutes.

My body was tired from long hours of outdoor activity I was unaccustomed to. But I found it easy to let go of my

*physical body because I wanted an answer to my prayer so
bad. I knew my meditation was deep because my whole
perception of the world completely changed. I felt like I had
something to give to everyone I talked to, and I gave that to
them.*

Meditation frees your consciousness. It enables you to have a fresh
and new outlook upon your life. Old situations are seen in a new light.
Comfortable patterns are challenged, habits rearranged. In the silence of
meditation, what we have denied comes to the forefront seeking admit-
tance, understanding, and release.

Those experiences that are not understood or misunderstood are
stored in the conscious mind. Since these memories are not understood
the individual is "unconscious" or not conscious of the ways he re-acts to
these misunderstood memories. Some of the memories may have been
completely buried in the brain to such a degree that the individual does
not even remember the actual experience yet re-acts to similar or non-
similar experiences in the present as if he was in the past. Thus, we have
people re-acting to the strangest or most non-threatening kinds of interactions with excuses that never quite hold true.

For example, suppose a parent tells their child continuously, "you'll
never amount to anything." The child may accept this statement as fact
since it came from the authority, his parent. As the child grows into an
adult he or she may continue to re-act with anger, fear, or avoidance to
innocent and even helpful or friendly situations. They may sabotage
themselves without even being consciously aware of how they do it. This
is the action of the unconscious part of the brain. Sometimes, strong
individuals become so determined to override or overcome the limitations
of their environment that they do whatever is required to change and
grow. They question their own set of attitudes, thoughts, habits, and
limitations. Identifying these limiting mental images they then go beyond
them proving the falsity of these limitations.

The unconscious is not to be confused with the Subconscious Mind.
The unconscious part of the brain is a function of the conscious mind and
physical brain. The Subconscious Mind, however, is a division of mind
and the abode of the soul.

In large part due to meditation, Damian is learning the difference
between these two.

> *My greatest meditation experience occurred when I was at commitment weekend on the College of Metaphysics' campus last October. The first night I was there we meditated as a group, chanting the Om.*
>
> *Dr. Dan (Condron) would initiate the chant and we would respond as a group. After 30-40 minutes of chanting we entered into meditation. I experienced the most peaceful meditation I have ever had. I went to commitment weekend with many burdens and cares on my mind, however, in meditation that night I found peace and joy. It was as if all of my worries were small and frivolous compared to the deep sense of calm I felt during that meditation. I felt as if I were balancing on a wire or the edge of a cliff where I had all of the control and centeredness that I would ever need.*
>
> *I'm not sure how long I stayed in that meditation, but I really didn't want to leave it.*

All of any person's worries are small and frivolous compared to the deep sense of peace, calm, love, and light one can experience in meditation. However, very few people realize this fact so they remain mired in their muddy thoughts of limitation and fear and worry. The meditator is not bound by these limitations. He experiences new levels of awareness and joy as meditation deepens. The meditator has access to a universal storehouse of knowledge, awareness, and wisdom, that the average person barely dreams of.

The one who is deeply involved in meditation learns to have the greatest balance in the world for they balance an outer, physical productive life filled with service to others, with an inner bliss filled, love encompassing, inner meditative life.

The best way to clean the fears, doubts, guilts, angers, and sorrows out of the unconscious part of the brain is to produce successes in your life. Go beyond your previously accepted limitations and by so doing, prove the falsity of your previous restrictions.

To produce success you must first imagine success. To produce greater successes you must image greater successes.

Most people only change when the pain of being the way they are becomes so great that the fear of change is less than the present experience of the pain. Fear is the greatest limitation because fear produces either a stopping of all forward motion or an avoidance of forward motion and an attempt to move backward. By reaching within one's mind to find the cause of the fear that cause can be changed and one's life transformed into a much larger and vast presentation of the Self.

With repeated expansion and movement beyond this fear-limitation the Self gradually or rapidly, depending on the degree of exercise of will power and application, moves beyond the fear limitation. Then this new, more expansive understanding of consciousness is added to the permanent soul growth called understanding.

Meditating on a regular basis supports and quickens the process of mental, emotional, and physical success. Meditation enables you to build understandings at a more rapid rate, for by learning to quiet the thoughts you are able to receive more from your environment.

If a person is talking to you, and your attention is wandering to something else, you receive little of what they have to say. If you give that person your full attention, you receive not only what they have to say you also receive that person's essence, intention, and whole thought. This gives you useful, workable knowledge that you can apply in your life. You have received knowledge that adds to what you already have so your decisions are better and your life is enhanced.

The brain is not the same thing as the Mind. The brain is a physical organ, a structure that the Conscious Mind utilizes in order to function in the physical environment. The brain may be likened to a computer that stores information for the Conscious Mind's day to day use. While the Conscious Mind is similar to or like the computer programmer or who directs the computer to do certain functions.

Brain pathways are built in the brain for the Conscious Mind to facilitate repeated actions. Brain pathways make repeated actions easier. However, brain pathways are always limited and raise a person very little above the level of an animal.

The Solar Plexus is the seat of the Conscious and Subconscious Minds. It is the area in the nervous system where the incoming energies of the Conscious and Subconscious Mind connect. If you are in a car and you go over a hill and the ground drops out from under you quickly as you go over the top of the hill you may feel "the bottom drop out of your stomach." Or if you are in an elevator and it moves suddenly you may notice a similar feeling. This is because the energies in your solar plexus have been disturbed, forced out of synchronization by external conditions. The mind may be compared to a light bulb in the way light radiates outward. The light of awareness moves from LIGHT to I AM to Superconscious Mind, then to the Subconscious Mind and lastly to the Conscious Mind and physical existence. The physical receives the least amount of the light of creation of all the levels of Mind. Similarly, a light bulb radiates light in all directions. As the light moves farther away from the bulb the light becomes more scattered and therefore dimmer. The same is true for a flashlight. The farther the beam of light moves from the flashlight the more diffused and therefore dimmer the light becomes.

The farther I AM moves from LIGHT the less awareness there is of one's true essence as LIGHT and less awareness of who you are as I AM. Until, finally, the Self having moved all the way out into the physical became engrossed in a physical body. The I AM is now engrossed as the conscious ego forgets where he came from and who he is. Most people have forgotten where they came from and who they are. If you ask people the question, "Who are you?", they will often reply, "I am a business man, a teacher, a farmer," or some other word that describes their profession or occupation rather than who they really are. Rarely, will a person say, "I am an eternal soul!" Even rarer still is the Self aware individual who can describe I AM to you, what their permanent understandings are, and the qualities of their soul.

A baby when first born functions from subconscious mind. The subconscious direction keeps the heart beating and breath working to bring oxygen into the lungs. These understandings are a part of subconscious memory and cause the physical body to function. As the child matures the conscious mind brings more and more of the body functions under conscious control and direction. This process of replacing subconscious mind use with conscious mind use and control occurs up to the age of 7 for most and 14 for some children. By then the subconscious mind is mostly covered over and the attention of the individual is completely engrossed in sensory experience. When this occurs the subconscious is covered over by the conscious mind and the individual is fully engrossed in the physical experience. The Self has forgotten she is a soul.

You have forgotten who you are and where you came from. Yet, by the age of 21, the end of the third seven year cycle, and the beginning of the fourth seven year cycle, the person finds out they still have a lot to learn. Whereas, as a teenager you think you know everything. The fourth seven year cycle is a time of striving to become compatible to and with your physical parents which is a reflection of the real inner urge to be like and compatible with your mental parent, your Creator. Due to this factor, individuals with a strong inner urge begin the search at this point to know who they are and how to cause their evolutionary and mental-spiritual growth to quicken.

The challenge for today's parents is to teach their children to meditate, to remember and interpret their dreams, and to practice and apply concentration in order that the doorway to the subconscious mind remains open as the child matures and develops his conscious mind. This process enables the individual to draw upon and utilize both the conscious and subconscious mind later as an adult. As the child ages he is then able to live his adult life as a genius making remarkable discoveries that benefit all mankind. These are the keys to having a world full of geniuses that lead humanity into a true Golden Age of Enlightenment.

Optimally, we would like to have the world full of geniuses and spiritually enlightened people. This is the destiny of mankind. The destiny of each individual is to become an enlightened being. An enlightened person is always a genius but a genius may not always be enlightened. Enlightenment is a process of building many understandings for the whole mind and the whole Self. While genius may come about when a person has developed one aspect of Self at the expense of other parts of Self. Genius may or may not be unbalanced. Enlightenment is always balanced forward motion, transformation and growth which develops the use of the whole mind.

The mind is a vehicle and tool for I AM to use. I AM uses the mind as spirit in Superconscious Mind. I AM uses the mind through the venue of soul in Subconscious Mind. I AM uses the mind as the physical body and Conscious Mind in the physical environment.

The Mind needs to be exercised just as a muscle needs to be exercised in order to be strong and efficient. The mind is like a tool or machine that must be used and taken care of in order to function properly when needed. The memory must be strengthened in order to know the past causes of your present situations and circumstances.

The attention must be strengthened through the use of concentration exercises in order to make the most of your present situation and to cause your present to be as you desire regardless of past situations and circumstances. The Conscious Mind is also strengthened by the act of imaging, often called visualization. The effective use of the imagination allows you to create in your mind's eye events, situations, circumstances, goals, and desires that have not yet occurred physically but will when there is enough activity to cause them to manifest.

Exercising the will also strengthens the Mind. Each person was given two free gifts when they were created as I AM: free will and identity. Everything else is earned. It is earned through will power and reasoning. We were created as individualized units of light with free will. It is the exercise of that free will that strengthens one's ability to create. The repeated and continuous exercise of the will through repeated and deliberate choice produces will power and eventually or rapidly creates success in any endeavor.

From the repeated exercise of the Mind and will an individual can create a new and greater security, confidence and authority within the Self. The action of directed change always produces an efficient use of the Mind.

The act of concentration harmonizes the Conscious and Subconscious Minds. By learning to focus your mind and direct your attention to one point the conscious mind is stilled allowing messages and communication from the inner mind to come through. Until the Conscious Mind is stilled to the point where environmental stimuli no longer distract and random thoughts no longer draw the attention away from the Real Self, there is little communication received from Subconscious Mind except through dream recall. Even then the person can refuse to remember his or her dreams, refuse to write them down, and refuse to interpret their own dreams which are messages from their subconscious mind.

The brain has a gland called the pituitary. The pituitary gland's duty is to interpret incoming energies and communication by translating this information into mental images already stored in the brain as memory. It receives and interprets dreams from Subconscious Mind and also messages from the five senses as they receive external stimuli which is then transferred through the sensory nerves to the brain. Dreaming utilizes a language of its own based on function. While the language of the physical universe or seventh level of Mind is based on form. The language of the Subconscious Mind is based on function.

The subconscious mind of someone who is male this lifetime is receptive while the conscious mind is created to be aggressive. The word aggressive as used in this book is defined as, initiating action. The subconscious mind of a female is aggressive which is not a bully, not forceful, but continually active while desiring forward motion. The female's conscious mind is designed to be receptive. Receptive used herein means to utilize the power of receptivity which is expectant non-action, listening and receiving. Receptivity in the conscious mind, whether you are male or female, is necessary for meditation.

In preparing for meditation it is important to have an ideal of what you want to become through meditation. Do you want to just relieve stress or do you want to achieve the great enlightenment? Do you desire to become a spiritually evolved being, a master teacher, and one who understands the essence and keys to Creation and desires to teach these to the world. Having an ideal in meditation causes there to be a singleness of awareness within the thinker so there is a connection and a connectedness with the higher realms of the Self as well as an awareness of all parts of Self.

As you dive deeper and ascend higher in meditation and experience the effects of the quietness and stillness of your own mind, remember to cause this to become a part of your every waking moment and movement. This will cause the type of awareness and enlightenment that you have an urge to accomplish.

The purpose of meditation is to build a relationship with your maker or Creator. This is the development of oneness with all of Creation as well as the full awareness and understanding of the interconnectedness of all of Creation and Self with all of Creation. This relationship you are building, constructing, and creating is one of compatibility.

The activity of meditation requires an individual to be able to have an awareness and the conscious thinking to be able to have control over quieting the sense receivers as well as the thoughts to reach a point of stillness or quietness within the Self. The quietness requires the quality of receptivity to be present within the individual.

Meditation enables one to communicate with the inner Self. Meditation then aids one in making conscious choices that are more closely in alignment with the Real Self or Inner Self.

1

What is the meaning of the word man?

The word *man* comes from the ancient Sanskrit word *Manu.* The word Manu means thinker. Man is the thinker. When the word is used in this book the thinker is indicated.

2

What is the conscious mind?

It is the mind used in conjunction with the physical senses.

3

What is the difference between the Conscious Mind and physical existence?

As given in the mind chart the Conscious Mind universally is physical existence. Individually you have a conscious mind that functions within the physical existence. Specifically your conscious mind uses your brain, physical body, and five senses to experience in and learn from the physical environment.

4

What is the power of the conscious mind?

The power of the conscious mind is reasoning.

5

What is the purpose of the Conscious Mind?

To glean permanent understandings.

6

What is the duty of the Conscious Mind?

To initiate continued activity upon desires.

7

Where is an individual's conscious mind?

The conscious mind is like a hologram that is most closely associated with the brain.

8

What is the brain?

An organ of the physical body.

9

Can the conscious mind go into Subconscious or Superconscious Mind?

No, but your conscious awareness can.

10

What is the purpose of physical existence in the Conscious Mind?

To build permanent understandings of the Universal Laws of Creation.

11

What is the goal of the individual's conscious mind?

To transcend the limitations of physical existence.

Conscious Mind Meditation

Meditation proceeds in deepening stages. Your first step is a conscious mind meditation. This is the process of learning to still your mind. If during a conversation with another person your mind is distracted, wandering, or thinking of something else you will miss most of what the other person is saying. In order to fully receive into yourself what the other person is saying you must stop the restless mind chatter. In order to fully receive what the other person is saying you must stop thinking. When you stop thinking and achieve the stage of no thought then you can receive fully what the other person is saying to you.

As long as there is prejudice, fear, doubt, judgement, envy or desire thoughts your mind is not quiet. The ability to receive fully is a very great power. In fact, receptivity, the ability to receive fully is one half the power of all creation.

In meditation you will receive from the inner levels and the inner divisions of Mind. As your ability to still your mind and receive increases so will your ability to receive in meditation increase.

Meditation is an act of receiving. To meditate is to still your mind and receive the answer to your prayer.

When preparing to meditate it is best at first to decide on a topic or question to ask. Decide on a question that you would like to have answered in meditation. Stating or offering your prayer or question or petition immediately prior to meditation gives you purpose and focus in then becoming receptive during meditation.

Stilling the mind requires some discipline and practice. Yet, anyone who has a strong desire can learn to achieve the still and quiet mind. A mind that is still is the beginning of peace. Until the still mind is achieved you will always be led around by the desires, whims, and habits of your conscious mind.

The conscious mind and brain are like an animal that must be disciplined and trained to obey you, the thinker's, commands. In fact, the brain which is a part of the physical body is the animal part of ourselves. In order to create happiness, joy, fulfillment, peace, and love in your life you must be the master of your physical body.

If you are going to meditate for fifteen minutes or more each day you will need to be able to tell your physical vehicle, your body, to do as you, the thinker, the soul inhabiting the body, desire. And your desire is for the physical body to remain still and give you no distractions during meditation. Just as you want your mind to be still so do you also want your physical body to be still.

In meditation you are to be quiet and your body is to be quiet. There should be no movement of your physical body during meditation. At first the body may re-act to this discipline by making you think that your arm itches and you have to scratch it. Do not scratch it. The itch will go away. The physical body may tell you that it is uncomfortable to sit still and in one position for 15 minutes. Ignore this. You have already made a commitment to sit in the meditation position for at least 15 minutes and you are not going to break your commitment. You will not allow your physical, animal, body to dictate to you, the thinker. You are better than that. You are the master of your life.

After a few days the twitches, itches, and aches will subside. You will experience fewer and fewer distractions from your body. This will free your mind to focus more and more on meditation. From this you see that discipline produces freedom. From meditation you will experience more freedom than you ever have in your life because you will master your own physical vehicle.

When you sit down to meditate sit either in a firm, straight backed-chair or preferably in a cross-legged position on the floor. The cross-legged position is preferable because it naturally stimulates the back to be straight. You will want your back to be straight and vertical during meditation. The head is to be held level on top of the neck. The head is not to be resting on your chest nor is it to be tilted backward. Rather your head needs to be delicately balanced at the top of the spine.

Breath is the factor that binds you to the physical body. The breath is what binds or ties you, the soul to the physical body. Learning to control the breath and the body enables you to move out of engrossment into viewing life as a soul and not a physical body. This is an aid to soul growth and spiritual development.

Before meditation sit in your meditation position and practice the following breathing exercise. Breathe in to a count of six, hold the breath to a count of three then exhale to a count of six. As you progress with this breathing exercise you will notice that you can slow your counting down and go longer and longer between breaths because your body is becoming more relaxed. Therefore, it is easier to remove your attention from the physical body and go within in meditation.

Since you always begin any journey where you are you will begin your meditation in the Conscious Mind.

Sit in a cross-legged position on the floor and face East. East is the direction of the rising sun and this serves as an aid to elevate your consciousness to a new level of awareness. You may, if you wish, sit in a straight backed chair with your feet flat on the floor during your meditation. The cross-legged position is preferred because it causes the back to straighten naturally. Your back needs to be erect and straight during meditation with the head balanced on the top of the spine neither tilting forward nor back. You do not want to go to sleep during meditation. You want to elevate your consciousness.

Next, close your eyelids and direct your gaze and your eyeballs upward, slightly. This is an aid to remember to elevate your consciousness. This helps to direct your attention to the inner Mind and the High Self. This tends to give you an upward focus on higher ideals and the higher divisions of Mind such as the Superconscious Mind. This also serves to slightly stimulate the pituitary or third eye, the eye of perception.

Next mentally state your petition, desire or prayer. This prayer may be about something you desire to learn, a way in which you desire to grow or it may be a thanksgiving for enlightenment, love, and bliss.

Now you are ready to begin your meditation.

In meditation, you are listening for the answer to your prayer or petition. In meditation which is a receptive experience you are receiving the peace, love, and bliss of the Creator. In meditation do not be so caught up in attempting to hear words that you fail to hear and appreciate the peace, love, and bliss you receive.

When the Conscious Mind is quiet and still there exists an alignment between Conscious, Subconscious, and Superconscious minds. Therefore, you may then receive from the inner minds.

At first meditate for 15 to 20 minutes once a day. Gradually, you may increase this to longer time periods.

At the end of meditation do not immediately jump or get up from your meditation. Open your eyes slowly and savor the delicious refreshment you have enjoyed which was your meditation. Hold and maintain this higher consciousness as you slowly come out of meditation and as you go about your daily, physical routine. Your goal is to make this higher consciousness, this peace, love, and bliss a permanent part of yourself that you have with you at all times and always, forever.

1

What do I do with all the thoughts and physical noises that keep coming into my head while I'm trying to concentrate on the Creator?

Let them pass through and give them no attention. It is just the conscious ego's way of trying to stay in control. As you give them no attention gradually your mind will become more and more still and you will have less and less extraneous thoughts. As you learn to go within you will find that less and less you notice your physical body and the noises and other incoming messages entering in through the five senses.

2

I can concentrate when I enjoy something or when I feel I have to concentrate, but I find it difficult to hold my attention still during meditation. How can I motivate myself to deepen my meditation?

By making it your strongest desire to know the Self, to know the Creator, and to know Creation. Then you will learn to enjoy meditation more than anything else in the whole, wide world. Find out all you can about the benefits of meditation. This is why I have included exciting meditation experiences of my students. By reading them you will stimulate a greater desire to gain the same benefits they have achieved from meditation and more.

3

What is correct posture for meditation? Sitting cross-legged is often recommended for meditation, however, I am not used to sitting this way and find it so uncomfortable that it is a significant distraction. I feel it takes away from, rather than adds to my experience. What is the benefit of sitting this way and is it necessary?

You may sit either cross-legged, with the back straight and neck and head erect or you may sit in a firm, straight backed chair. I prefer you sit cross legged on the floor because it is much easier to keep your back straight and head erect. This allows the energies to flow freely and for the Kundalini energy to rise up the spine.

Before you begin meditation do some stretching exercises. This will loosen your joints and stretch your muscles. When you sit to meditate, if you are limber place your right foot on top of your left leg or vice-versa. This is called the half lotus position. It will help insure your back stays straight and cause less numbing of the legs than the full lotus. With practice you will notice this effect less and less.

4

Should my head stay elevated during meditation or drop?

The head needs to be balanced on top of the neck. The face should be facing forward. The head is not to be resting on the chest or tilted backwards. When the head is perfectly balanced on the neck there is no tension so it is easier to remove the attention from the physical head and physical body. This position also enables the Kundalini energy to rise up the spinal column, through the head and out the top of the head and through the crown chakra. The crown chakra has been referred to as the thousand petaled lotus in Indian literature.

5

Is it best to meditate in the same place every time?

Yes, because you impregnate that place with the deep meditation aura, thought form, and vibration. Then when you meditate in that same spot next time it will be easy to return to the depth of meditation you achieved before instead of trying to spend the whole meditation time getting to your previous depth. Instead you can build on what you achieved in previous meditations and progress rapidly. Have a special room or corner of a room that you use only for meditation. Meditate at the same time each day. Remove all distractions from the room such as radio or television sounds, smells, etc. Face east as this is the direction of the rising sun. Let each meditation cause the dawning of a new awareness and an expanded consciousness within you.

6

Can I meditate with soft music playing in the background?

It is possible for a master to meditate under almost any situation but very few people can do it. For best meditation you want to eliminate all distractions. The fact that you would want music playing while you are meditating indicates you are still attached to and engrossed in the senses. In this case the sense of hearing. Incense can be a distraction from meditation because it draws you to the physical odor, the smell. Remember, in meditation, the first goal is to still your mind and remove your attention from the physical body and the five senses. To go to the inner levels of Mind you must remove your attention from the physical body and physical environment.

7

What happens to the physical body when you meditate?

It relaxes. Tension departs. Meditation relaxes the muscles and stimulates the nervous system. Meditation causes there to be more life and life force within the whole system. Meditation causes a balancing of the bodily system. When you meditate you relax all systems of the body giving them a much needed rest. You also release all stress and all unproductive or limiting thoughts and attitudes. This leads to a healing and rejuvenation of the entire body. Because the body is relaxed the consciousness of the meditator can depart and go beyond the confines of the physical body.

8

What are the mental effects of meditation?

A calm, peaceful, focused mind. A fulfillment and a knowing that what you are doing is right and is good for your eternal soul. A definite knowing that you are important and have value and are on this earth for a very important reason and with a very specific purpose.

9

How old do children have to be to start teaching them meditation?

Old enough to sit still, close their eyes, and still their mind.

10

How do I cause a transcendental meditation experience so that I can have a strong desire to regain that experience and more in meditation?

Practice meditation diligently, every day, with an open heart and an open mind and in a thankful and receptive state. Read this book, especially the dramatic experiences related by students about their meditation.

Chapter Three

Receptivity

Perhaps the most important factor in learning of any kind is the ability to receive. When you excel at receiving you are able to receive all the joy, love, goodness, and learning the world has to offer. Without the ability to receive you are alone, isolated, and separate. The more enlightened you become the more you are able to receive all the joy, bliss, peace, universal love, knowledge, wisdom, and understanding the universe has to offer.

There are two main principles at work in the universe. They are the aggressive principle and the receptive principle. The aggressive principle works with the quality of giving while the receptive principle functions through the action of receiving. The aggressive principle manifests itself as initiating activity and in the masculine presentation. The receptive principle manifests itself as the drawing power of the feminine expression.

In meditation we strive to make full use of the receptive principle. In meditation we desire to surrender our small conscious mind and conscious ego to our expansive High Self, our Real Self which is much closer to LIGHT and the Creator.

In meditation, you do not go someplace, someplace comes to you. As your consciousness expands and grows gradually, or quickly, you come to encompass the world, the universe, and all of Mind. Then you are one with the Cosmos because you are where it is and you understand, know, and recognize that creation is where it is.

You can remain isolated and alone all your life or you can receive the abundance, joy, bliss, fulfillment, and enlightenment the Universe and Superconscious Mind have to offer.

Over the last 20 years I have taught thousands of people. I have perceived that everyone has walls of mental protection around themselves that they have spent many years forming since infancy and childhood. Meditation enables you to build the security and strength needed to let these mental, emotional and physical walls of isolation and so-called protection down. Only then do the wonders of creation and enlightenment come pouring in. Only then do you experience a greater love than you have ever experienced before. Then you can receive the bliss, love, LIGHT, peace, and oneness of Superconscious Mind and all of Creation.

No one is keeping you from experiencing happiness in life. You are blocking the universal happiness that always is. Meditation is your tool, your vehicle for letting down these walls and opening up yourself to the Supreme Eternal LIGHT and love.

Do not try to grasp a foreign or new idea. Instead receive it into your whole being. Grasping is not receiving. Grasping is akin to taking. Receive a thought or idea, then apply it and use it.

By giving freely and without restriction every day and in every way you will stop trying to protect yourself and learn to receive. Jim is a Canadian who studies with SOM through correspondence. His following meditation experience, which occurred January first while celebrating the annual Universal Hour of Peace, illustrates the power of giving.

Before my hour of peace began, I started with an opening projection. My stated ideal was to live peaceably; my purpose was to become a peaceful person; my activities, every day to think peaceably and live in peace.

For the first forty minutes I chanted the Sanskrit "Om Namaha Shivaya" – I bow to the Lord who is the Inner Self. With each incantation I thought of someone I knew, wishing and sending them peace. These folks included friends, family, and also those I have had differences with. During the final 20 minutes I chanted the Universal "OM" and joined in spirit with like-minded metaphysicians around the globe projecting my desire for peace for humanity.

I concluded the hour reciting out loud, the Prayer of St. Francis of Assisi.

"Lord make me an instrument of Thy peace;
Where there is hatred, let me sow love;
Where there is injury, pardon;
Where there is doubt, faith;
Where there is despair, hope;
Where there is darkness, light;
Where there is sadness, joy.
Oh Divine Master, grant that I may not so much
seek
To be consoled as to console;
To be understood as to understand;
To be loved as to love;
For it is in the giving that we give,
It is in the pardoning that we are pardoned;
It is in dying to self that we are born again to eternal
life."

*Throughout the hour I experienced a sense of connectedness, of
being one with all and one purpose.*

The prayer of St. Francis of Assisi is focused around the quality of giving.
The benefits of giving, eternal life, is also given in the prayer.

The vehicle of meditation provides a way for the Conscious Mind to
receive more and to have a greater capacity to receive. Then the Conscious Mind admits it is greater than before and has a greater ability and
capacity to receive. You can come to expect and receive larger results
from your efforts. The Conscious Mind admits it is greater and more
expansive than it was before meditation.

The following are steps to causing productive change:

1. *Discipline your conscious mind*
2. *Focus on the productive*
3. *Cause creations to be larger*

One is most capable of receiving when the Mind is still and the body
is still. Receptivity is impossible without stillness. To the degree the
Mind is still is also the degree to which receptivity is possible. Receptivity is one half the power of creation.

Some people think they will only be successful if they are constantly doing something. They work themselves into an early grave and never achieve the success they desire because they either don't know how to receive or are afraid of receiving.

A student I know is a good example of this. At the College of Metaphysics we have our meals together and we often discuss the student's application and progress in learning. Once there was a student who used eating as a protection device. No matter what was being discussed this girl would just keep on eating. As long as we were at the table she would keep on eating. Even if we were at the table for more than one hour she used or more accurately *misused* food as a distraction because she was afraid of receiving.

This woman also is a taker. She grabs things. This is the way people who are afraid of receiving act. They grab and take things. People who are takers never receive. This is why they are skinny. They are skinny because their body does not receive most of the nourishment of the food. The food goes into their mouth, then into their stomach, through their intestines and out of the body without ever being assimilated. The calories, the minerals, the vitamins, the proteins, are poorly received by the body because the mind is afraid of receiving. The physical body, and its function, always reflects the state of consciousness of its owner. This student blocks receiving and her physical body reflects this. So do her interactions with others. She will say something and walk off into another room because she is afraid of receiving the response to her statement. She is afraid of receiving truth and so she closes off by physically removing herself or distracting her mind with physical objects such as food. She eats more food than anybody at the table, yet never gains any weight because the food is never assimilated. She is skinny as a rail, with little endurance even though she is a young adult.

The whole power of the world and mankind's future depends on receptivity.

Receptivity permits you to receive into yourself understanding you did not previously have. This enables expansion of consciousness. When the jar of your mind is full of the water of consciousness, the jar of your mind expands to receive more.

In meditation always prepare to and expect to receive something greater into yourself than you previously achieved and used.

Meditation is a receptive process. The whole purpose of meditation is to receive the consciousness which is greater and more expansive into yourself. Gradually or quickly through this process your mind expands into first Subconscious and then Superconscious Mind and fills the entire universe.

Then you come to know I AM.

Some people falsely believe that to truly experience stillness is to have nothing in the mind. This is not the case. To truly experience stillness is to achieve a state of complete receptivity.

Passivity and complete receptivity are not the same. Passivity is doing nothing and shows lack of control.

When a person is receptive to you it is one of the best experiences you can ever have. Receptivity is beautiful, lovely, exquisite. In meditation, you are to be receptive.

Passivity, however, is the refusal to move from the unpleasant, uncomfortable, or unproductive place you are. Passivity is the refusal to move and cause forward motion.

Many and perhaps most of the reasons people refuse to change and grow is fear. Fear stops motion and thereby, leads to passivity.

Once a student refused to change and grow. He held onto the past and was constantly talking about the past. When he was not talking about the past he was trying to get something from whoever happened to be in the immediate environment. This in turn made him so passive he became physically sick. Presently, he is learning to face his fear, let go the limitations it produces and go beyond this to a new, more expansive, and healthier way of living and being.

Whether your attention is in the past, present, or future is a function of where you choose to place your attention. Robert, a lifelong meditator, is discovering the depth of meaning in this simple truth: you are where your attention is.

During meditation my attention was pretty well controlled and the sensation of freedom was, as always, glorious. My latest Intuitive Health Analysis told me that I have too much attention in the past and my focus is being brought back to the present more and more.

I am still waiting to meet the Creator, whom I still imagine
to be in a humanoid shape. I am experiencing a light and love
now in my meditations that is wonderful and it may just be that
I am truly experiencing my Creator. Maybe it is my love and
light as a microcosm of the whole. I do not know but I am as
curious as all get out.

Some people fear that by achieving this stillness of mind and receptivity they will lose all sense of who they are and lose themselves and, in essence, lose control. This is not true. This fear can stifle the natural sense of curiosity that urges us toward Self discovery and Self transformation.

As you are willing to pursue the state of stillness and receptivity you will come to know the truth.

During meditation the meditator needs to quiet and still the thoughts of the mind. To obtain stillness in the mind is not to have nothing in the mind nor is it to stop the mind rather it is to have a state of complete receptivity.

Learn to be more open and share your thoughts and feelings. Cause there to be a willingness to be vulnerable. This does not mean one is weak. It does provide an opportunity to receive and therefore learn, for without receiving there is no learning. Teaching is an aggressive process while learning is a receptive process. Teaching is showing. Teaching is giving while learning is a function of receiving.

Receptivity provides the self with many benefits. By disciplining the mind one learns to:

1. *Still the mind*
2. *Listen to one's inner desires*
3. *Respond according to one's Inner Desires.*

Learn to relish the ability to receive. It is by receiving that one is able to

1. *Birth wisdom*
2. *Evolve*
3. *Become rich and wealthy in all ways.*

Skepticism occurs when the mind is closed. Skepticism is related to rejection of authority or rebelliousness. Skepticism occurs when the mind is closed and when reasoning is lessened.

When the mind is open there is an increase and enhancement of awareness that benefits the Self and others in one's environment immediately.

Robert, an electronics engineer in his late 50's, has been meditating daily for many years. Like many in his field, he outwardly chose his career for practical reasons that are actually rooted in very spiritual ones. Meditation has helped him dispel the limits imposed by his skepticism while revealing to him a deeper meaning and purpose to his life. He describes one of these experiences in this way:

> *In detail, I went through the preparation for meditation which included the "Lord's Prayer" and a desire to know my Heavenly Father. I went as deep as Hong Sau (a spiritual practice employed commonly in Eastern disciplines and taught in the School of Metaphysics) will take me.*
>
> *I was floating over 'fields' – Elysian Fields comes to mind, although I'm not sure why – they were like physical fields. They were more like fields of light and clouds – light and airy. There was a wonderful sense of freedom and a connection with everything. My attention was pretty well controlled but not to the point that I am satisfied.*
>
> *After meditation, I talked with Dr. Gerry (DeMate Hatcher) about this dissatisfaction and she suggested that I be curious.*
>
> *Curious! I thought I was curious. But curiosity was lacking during this experience. I just was.*

By controlling, focusing, and directing his attention Robert was able to experience the freedom of his mind. The Subconscious and Superconscious Minds are freedom and have freedom. Because of this your true nature is freedom. It is only in the physical, engrossed life that we experience restriction and limitation. Focusing and directing the attention through concentration enables the meditator to expand the consciousness infinitely which is freedom.

The light and love experienced come first from the Creator, the Supreme, the Eternal and then through the divisions and levels of Mind. When the attention is freed from the limitations of the physical body and conscious mind the Self is free to soar. This was the experience of flying.

To experience true freedom is to experience and have a true connection with everything. When you are truly connected with the whole universe then the whole universe and everything in it is at your service to use to create. This is for the benefit of yourself and all of humanity for as you progress and grow in soul awareness you have more to offer others.

It is the quality of receptivity that will draw to you all that you desire. The action of receiving gives you the opportunity to be filled and fulfilled.

In order to improve your receptivity, view giving as a joyous opportunity and expect to receive.

Constantly refusing to receive causes a perpetual drain on the Self. Rebelliousness rejects. It pushes away. It is contrary to receiving. As long as you are rebelling you are fighting against something, someone, and yourself. As long as you are fighting against something you can not receive for you have a protective wall around yourself. You need to expand your consciousness. Meditation is the receptive power that will enable you to do so.

When your mind is still and you are receptive there is no judgement for judging, judgement and pre-judice are all impediments to receiving and therefore, learning. One needs to receive instead of judge.

When there is the openness to receive there is receptivity. When there is receptivity there is the possibility for communication. When communication exists through receptivity and openness, the conscious mind can more closely imitate, replicate, or duplicate the plan of oneness with no separation held in Superconscious Mind.

The reason one must surrender the ego outwardly to the teacher is that to evolve one must freely give to all and therefore be a part of all. This is not possible as long as you have a wall of protection around yourself. If you want to be able to trust other people you must first learn to trust yourself. The way to build self trust is to communicate completely and fully.

There is a need on the part of everyone to learn to give one's full energy to something greater than the Self whether it is the Creator or humanity. To do this you must surrender the stubbornness. When you feel inadequate it causes your conscious mind to shut down. Then you are not capable of receiving and processing information.

Remember meditation is not an aggressive action. Meditation uses the receptive faculty.

Some people believe there is an obligation that goes along with receiving. Therefore these people push other people away from themselves. When they are in a position to touch, be it mental, emotional, or physical such a person closes off and pushes other people away. The isolation that results keeps you entrapped in a physical body with physical separateness.

Remember, receiving and receptivity are very powerful. Receiving is not vulnerability. It is just the opposite. Being closed off is vulnerable. The universal nature of intimacy is full receiving and bringing to one another the awareness of the inner self and the desire to aid each other.

Some people mistakenly think of receptivity as submission. Receptivity and aggressiveness are not an interplay of submission and dominance. Receptivity gives nourishment, growth, and love. To produce the understanding of receptivity you need stillness within Self and mind.

Complete or pure receptivity is always open. It has to be in order to receive. In addition, receptivity has a strong drawing power.

The two qualities of receptivity are:

1. *openness*
2. *drawing*

The beauty of receptivity is the quality of openness.

The power of receptivity is the quality of drawing to itself. Drawing might be described as a pulling power but pulling does not adequately describe the exquisite joy nor the subtle influence found in receptivity.

Each person needs to vibrate at the highest frequency possible thereby becoming a drawing and guiding Light to those who also possess these higher frequencies but have not learned to be consciously aware of them, or to harness and use them productively this lifetime.

When you touch someone do you just physically touch them with your finger or hand or just brush them with your body, or do you touch them also with your soul?

In Superconscious Mind everyone touches everyone else. Notice I did not say every-body, I said everyone because you do not have a physical body in Superconscious Mind. You must therefore learn to like and love yourself and learn to like and love others. Otherwise you will not be willing to touch everyone all the time and so you won't be able to exist in Superconscious Mind.

This is why service is so important as part of the process of existence in Superconscious Mind. Service is giving to others and therefore, loving others. When you give to others and love others there is no wall of separation between yourself and others. When you give freely you have the opportunity to receive freely.

View giving as a joyous opportunity and expect to receive. In order for any creation to occur there must be love as well as receptivity. Each person has a particular place in the universe. Through service you not only discover your place in the universe but you are also able to lead the kind of life that will bring you to a higher consciousness.

1

*How can I receive the most from my petition or prayer
in meditation so that I can explain this to students?*

By stilling the body and stilling the mind. Practice
each day and each week sharing your valuable inner
life experiences with others. Teach others what you
are learning.

2

*How can you aggressively hold your attention on a
thought and at the same time be receptive to receiving
an expanded awareness of that thought?*

Let's go beyond the limitations of the words aggressive and receptive and experience the mental image.
Place your attention on a thought, focus on that
thought and the mind begins to slow down because
your attention is not racing from one thought to
another. As you learn to train your mind to slow
down you have greater awareness of your thoughts.
From that you next begin to be aware of who it is
behind the thoughts. Then you begin to have self
awareness or awareness of the Real Self behind the
thoughts and the one causing the thoughts. At that
time you have a great freedom that surpasses anything you have experienced before. You are no
longer a victim to your thoughts. Your mind is free
to expand into first Universal Consciousness and
then Cosmic Consciousness.

3

Sometimes I hear a voice in meditation. Is that my inner self, my inner voice or is it communication from another entity?

You will know your Inner Self for you will experience a greater peace, love, and joy that you have ever experienced before. This is not necessarily true of listening to another entity.

4

Sometimes images appear very clearly and at other times, you think everything is the same and you desire great things and nothing happens. What's the cause?

The hallmark of a good meditation is not whether you have received images or not. The mark of an excellent meditation is the peace you experience in and after meditation. If you get caught up in wanting to have mental images in meditation then you will remain in the conscious mind. You will be daydreaming. Go beyond the conscious mind. Learn to receive the love, peace, and LIGHT from the High Self.

5

The images I receive in meditation are sometimes fuzzy and unclear. What can I do to interpret them and figure out what I have received?

The goal of meditation is not to receive images. The goal of meditation is to still the mind and listen.

6

How can I get to a point in my meditation that I can clearly communicate with the Creator?

Prayer is your time to talk to the Creator. Meditation is your time to listen. Do not try to force the Eternal to talk to you. Rather surrender your small conscious ego so that you no longer have any blockages in yourself to receiving. Learn to completely still the mind. Only then will you be able to truly listen for the answer to your prayers and supplications. Then you will hear the Creator.

7

Sometimes I receive pictures, sometimes a voice, and sometimes actual words. Are all forms of messages from the same level of consciousness, or do different levels generate different types of messages, in different "packages"?

You are thinking physically instead of mentally or spiritually. You expect to hear physical words and see physical images but neither of these exist in the inner levels of Mind particularly the Superconscious Mind. Therefore desire to receive peace, joy, understanding, Light, willingness to serve, and desire to serve.

8

When I am experiencing something new how can I accept it and get the most of the moment?

By stilling the mind and completely receiving the experience into yourself. Approach each experience with the wonder and joy of a child, an infant.

9

When you have an answer to your question, what would be a good step for using the awareness?

First write the answer down on a sheet of paper shortly after finishing meditation. Next make a commitment to use it in your daily life. Third, decide how you are going to use the answer on a daily basis for your benefit and the benefit of others.

10

How can I receive the voice of God?

Through the quiet mind is the Creator known. See, I stand at the door and knock. "I" is your own High Self.

Chapter Four

Commitment to Self, and Superconscious Mind

When Lyle, at 35, began meditating he experienced what he recalls as probably his greatest meditation.

During one of my first meditations I experienced what I believe was an alignment of the levels of mind.
It was a time when I was aware of all in Creation.
I was alive and aware of love. Love present everywhere in everything.
I experienced something beyond the limits of the physical realms as I know it. Tremendous love and expansion. Love and expansion vibrating.

A surveyor by trade, Lyle glimpsed in that moment what is, and brought back the awareness as memory of what can be.

Those who experience superconscious meditation realize awareness of all Creation. You experience Self as full of life and vitality or more alive than ever before. It is as if you have been blind and now you can see or as if someone has lifted the veil that kept you from seeing more than a few feet in front of you. Your consciousness is expanded and you experience love and expansion.

This kind of meditation experience, like Lyle's, tells you what you can look forward to as you grow, learn and expand your consciousness until this high level of awareness becomes permanently yours. Until at last this great Love is permanently yours and your Light is so great that there is no more darkness within the Self and you become a shining beacon of light, a shining sun that lights the way for all others to find their way to true enlightenment, cosmic consciousness.

Such consciousness is revealed to one who is committed.

Without commitment, expansive creation is almost impossible. Without commitment expansion of consciousness is impossible. With commitment the thinker is able to manifest into the physical, his greatest most heartfelt desires. Commitment = Steadfastness = Endurance.

Without commitment you will never learn to concentrate. With commitment you can and will learn to concentrate and meditate. Through commitment you will build the capacity to go into the deepest levels of mind exploring your essence and the nature of creation.

Without commitment you will stay the same, never changing. The only change will be when you are forced to change by outside circumstances determined by someone or something else. With creation you become the Creator. You cause change and growth within yourself and the environment in which you live.

What is commitment and why is it so powerful? The answer lies in the ingredients that make up commitment. The first ingredient is a mental image. In order to have commitment one must have something to be committed to. Thus, a mental image becomes a goal or an ideal. A goal is usually physical, whereas an ideal is mental or spiritual. The word ideal comes from the word idea. Now an idea is a mental image or picture. Let's say you have formulated an idea of what you are going to do today. That idea is a mental image or mental picture. If you then write down your idea on paper you will notice that you have transformed the mental image from a mental image to a symbolic word form of alphabetical letters.

For any successful creation to occur there are three factors necessary. These three factors are ideal, purpose and activity. At any level of meditation whether beginner, advanced or adept one needs to have an ideal for meditation. An ideal is an image of what you want to become and where you want to be as an evolved soul.

Everyone needs something to move toward. Therefore, we create physical goals as markers of where we have come from and where we are going. Commitment entails clearly identifying these markers or goals and moving toward them consistently every day.

Creation is a building process and this means there must be effort applied daily to our creations in order to achieve the desired results. We experience a regular earthly cycle of day and night. The physical body of man, the thinker, has evolved to utilize this cycle. This is why daily application is necessary in order to achieve excellence in anything. Once the activity is memorized then visualization can be applied to enhance the activity and effort. Goals give you physical direction. They provide a physical object or subject to focus upon and move towards. An ideal provides a spiritual or mental subject that you want to become. You can achieve a goal without changing whereas ideals, when applied, are always life transforming and consciousness expanding. A goal, by being physical, provides little motivation while an ideal provides inspiration which is the highest form of motivation. This is why when formulating a goal it is important to have a purpose also. Purpose provides motivation for your goals.

Constantly hold in mind an ideal for yourself of not just what you want to do with your life but more importantly, what you want to be, what you want to become, and the qualities you desire to build within Self.

The next step is to create and find your purpose in life. Everyone has a purpose in life. To find your purpose in life, meditate and listen.

To serve your purpose in life:

1. *Identify what you know to be true based upon what you have made a part of yourself.*

2. *Place yourself in a position of service, teaching others what you have learned.*

Paul's reflections about meditation exemplify the need for, pursuit of, and realization of purpose.

After a lengthy stretch of commitment to meditation when I first started, I lapsed for some reason. I was hesitant in restarting, in re-committing, because I thought I would have a struggle getting back into it.

When I finally sat down again, I just did it. Meditating on "courage", I had the clearest most expansive and illuminating meditation to that point. There was a welcoming home that I experienced.

I learned the value of regular practice, as well as commitment, courage, and trust in myself.

Commitment is one of the greatest qualities anyone can have. Commitment is also one of the greatest qualities any meditator can have. No Olympic athlete ever achieved success without regular, consistent, practice. No great musician ever knew greatness without regular discipline and practice. Paul is an outstandingly talented individual, yet without commitment his talents would be wasted, left to stagnate. By putting his creative mind into action, Paul created a greater purpose for his meditation. This provided him with the motivation needed to go deeper into meditation.

Greatness, knowing, understanding, wisdom, and love – all are born out of the persistent desire to know and the commitment to do so. Meditate every day without fail. Meditate twice on weekends or when you are remembering that you are bringing the day of full enlightenment that much closer.

Words describe mental images and the mind operates from mental images or pictures. This is why the mind, and the thinker who is a mental being, always needs goals and ideals to guide him. There needs to be one major ideal in life motivating one to go beyond their limitations. There must also be daily, weekly, monthly, yearly and lifetime goals to give direction and encouragement to the self. Each person needs to see progress in his life in order to gain a sense of satisfaction and fulfillment.

Commitment is of utmost importance in the step by step, day by day, week by week improvement in your ability to meditate. Each day you need to have a goal for your meditation of going deeper then the previous day. If this does not happen one day rest assured that by being committed to your meditation every day you will have a breakthrough. Today, tomorrow, or the next day your meditation will deepen. The eager student's meditation will deepen either quickly or gradually over time depending upon effort, receptivity and, past permanent understandings. The key is consistency and commitment.

Be committed to meditating the same time and place every day. However don't be so stubborn and inflexible that you can't meditate at a different time of day or different room or under a different tree than you are used to. Your true commitment is to meditate every day no matter what the conditions and still be able to go deeper within than you did on the previous day. Learn to be stronger than your environment. Do not allow the limitations of your environment to determine your limitations or your spiritual progress.

You must be more powerful then your environment. You must learn to create your desires, goals, and ideals no matter what is going on around you for you have free will, the creative imagination, and a mind directed by the thinker, you.

Daily practice of commitment as exhibited through your activity overpowers, overrides, and diminishes any limitation you may have whether real or imagined in your head. Be committed, for with commitment you will become the Christ or the Buddha. You will become a being of light, the en-light-ened one. You will become the shining beacon of light that illuminates the path of awareness for others. You move ahead of most of mankind in your quest for greater awareness. You join the spiritually evolved family of intuitive, spiritual beings.

Commitment is intimately connected with and the driving force behind movement of a strong thought form from the third level of mind to manifestation into the physical existence.

Commitment entails regularity. The body functions on a 24 hour cycle as does the planet Earth. The two are synchronized. This is why true progress is intimately connected with daily repetition. In order to improve and develop a high degree ability, capability and facility one must practice daily. If you want to improve and develop anything you must practice at least once and preferably more each day.

To become proficient in meditation requires you meditate at least once every day. The people who are the very best in their field constantly have their attention and activity on what they want to do and become. Albert Einstein constantly thought about the Universe and how all the different parts of the Universe work together as one. Nicola Tesla, perhaps America's greatest scientific genius, constantly thought of electricity and other forms of energy. He would build machines and inventions to harness, use, and distribute that energy for mankind's benefit. Highly developed, spiritual people constantly think of how they can bring the energy of the Superconscious Mind into the physical for the benefit of mankind.

You too must constantly consider and employ ways to raise your consciousness. The greatest of these is meditation. Meditation provides definite results. Meditation aids in relaxation. Meditation helps to release stress. Meditation has been known to help heal all sorts of dis-ease and dis-orders. This is because during deep meditation the meditator releases and goes beyond the Conscious Mind first to Subconscious and later into Superconscious Mind. By going beyond the brain and Conscious Mind the meditator leaves behind for a short time habits, limitations, and, unproductive thought attitudes that are the cause of the individual's dis-order and the cause is temporarily removed. The degree to which the greater awareness gained in meditation is retained afterwards is the degree to which the dis-order is permanently eliminated.

As the benefits of meditation are retained more and more as a part of the Self in the waking Conscious Mind, gradually or quickly the limitations of Self, including dis-ease, are overcome. All limitations can be overcome with the power born of meditation since all power comes from and derives from the inner levels of mind. All power in the inner levels of Mind derives from LIGHT and the power of LIGHT derives and comes from the CREATOR. Therefore, it is each person's duty to productively and creatively aid Self and others thereby returning this used creative energy to the Creator from whence it came.

Have you ever tried putting drops of ink or colored dye in a bucket of water one drop at a time? Perhaps you did this when you were a child. If you notice the first drop did not make much difference in the color of the water. It still looked clear. After putting a second, third, fourth, and fifth drop of red ink in the bucket of clear water you may begin to notice the water begins to have a very, slight, pink cast to it. By the time ten drops of red ink have been added to the jar or bucket the clear water in it has taken on a definite pink color. Further drops of red ink make the water darker and darker until gradually or quickly, depending on how the quantity of red ink, the water turns from light pink to dark pink to red.

The image of ink drops used in the water may be used as an analogy for the way thoughts placed in Subconscious Mind begin to move into and manifest into a person's daily life (see *Diagram 6*). Remember, things evolve from success, not failure. Therefore, consistency in activity and commitment create progress. Progress is more important than success. With progress you will always, sooner or later, have success.

Just as one drop of red ink has little noticeable effect on the bucketful of clear water so does one random, weak, or scattered thought have little

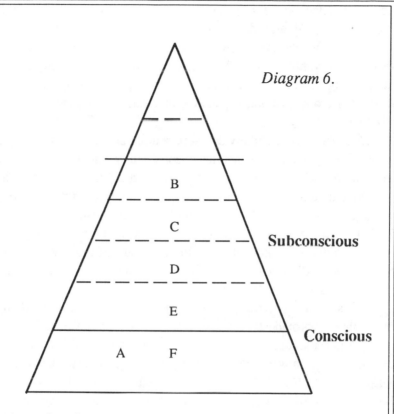

Diagram 6.

A = *a thought pictured or imaged by you in your conscious mind.*

= *the movement of your thought into Subconscious Mind.*

B = *your imaged thought having moved into the deepest level of Subconscious Mind.*

BCDE = *the movement of your thought-image through the levels of Subconscious Mind, gathering mind substance in order to form the physical result of your thought.*

F = *the manifestation of your thought image into physical existence.*

noticeable effect on the world at large. However, when the thought has been repeated day after day, week after week, month after month, and year after year, the cumulative effect is enormous. And when your thoughts are combined with like thoughts of like minds the effects can be earth-changing either for the better or worse depending upon whether the thought is productive and expansive, or limited, unproductive, and restrictive.

One who meditates daily develops a more powerful and productive mind. The person who meditates consistently and is committed to meditation produces strong thought forms that overcome all limitations and limited attitudes. Such a one helps humanity to manifest a better place for everyone to live in peace and harmony. Instead of drops in a bucket, the mind becomes powerful enough with the focused, expansive thought to place a continual, committed, stream of thought forms into Subconscious Mind that manifest as a continual steam of earth-changing improvement for the Self and others.

In a similar way several minds working together with like thought images and goals or ideals can cause a thought form placed in Subconscious mind to gather substance more quickly, grow more rapidly, and manifest as a part of our outward, physical, existence more rapidly. In just such a fashion 2, 3, 5, 10, 100, or 1000 people putting drops of red ink into a bucket of clear water will cause the water to turn pink and then red much quicker than one person working alone.

The power is in a still, focused, directed mind and a committed Self. The power is in many committed minds working together.

Meditation causes one's full power to spring forth. As the Conscious Mind is stilled, it comes into alignment with first the Subconscious Mind. Following this the conscious and subconscious minds come into alignment with the Superconscious Mind. The inner minds provide the Self with power that seems superhuman to the average person. This is the power to create. This is the power to mold and change the physical existence for the better and truly create peace on earth.

Meditation needs to be practiced on a daily basis not every other day or once a week or once a month. This is because the physical body works on a 24 hour cycle as does nature and the planet Earth. To learn to excel in any area or endeavor one must practice every day. If you want to be a good basketball player you must practice every day preferably for at least one hour. If you want to be a good physicist you must think and practice physics every day. If you want to be a good writer you must write every day and so it is with meditation.

The physical body must be trained to sit still every day for your body needs to remain still and motionless during meditation. The conscious mind also must be disciplined every day to become still and quiet. Only when the conscious mind is stilled and the thoughts cease to distract, is the conscious mind capable of receiving from the inner subconscious and superconscious mind.

Meditation needs to be practiced every day. Progress in developing any skill, talent, ability, proceeds from daily practice and application. I say application because what you gain in meditation needs to be applied, used, and carried on throughout the day in everything you do. A child does not learn to walk by attempting to walk once a month. A child does not learn to walk by practicing walking once a week. A child tries to walk every day. He may fall down may times every day but each time he will get up and practice walking again. A child continues to practice walking every day many times each day, until he can walk. A child never thinks "it is impossible, I will never be able to walk." The child accepts the fact that he will learn to walk and he wants to practice a lot so he can learn quickly. The child knows without a doubt that he will learn to walk because he has seen mommy and daddy walk and he wants to be like them. His efforts are commitment in action.

You practice commitment by being regular and consistent in your activity and by imaging the highest you could imagine in soul growth. There is no freedom until there is commitment and now you are gaining greater freedom.

Commitment also produces clear thinking. When you have decided what you are going to do and are committed to it there are fewer distractions in your mind and in your life. The mind becomes focused on the goal. This focus produces a clarity of perception within the thinker.

At the College of Metaphysics where I reside and teach, I often give students the opportunity to practice specific activities of commitment that lead to achievement of a specific present goal. For example, there may be some lessons, booklets, or pamphlets that need to be collated and stapled. I will ask my student how many lessons, booklets, or pamphlets he or she will commit to putting together each day until the whole printing is completed. The choice of how many, whether 10, 20, 30, or more, is the student's. What I as their teacher expect is that once they have chosen the daily goal or quantity to be collated, each day that student will be sure to do at least the amount he or she is committed to. If he says 10, I expect 10 or more to be done each day. If he says twenty then that is what I expect.

Commitment is a very powerful tool for with commitment you can accomplish anything. I want my students to learn that they can accomplish anything. I want them to learn how they can achieve their greatest goals, ideals, and desires, and most importantly, enlightenment.

Commitment is a very important key to achievement. Anyone who is reading this book has a desire to know Self and to reach for enlightenment. Commitment is a key that must be applied in order for true and rapid progress to occur.

Please learn to be committed to meditation every day. Begin with 15 minutes every day. Then, when you are ready, challenge yourself to 20 or 30 minutes of meditation every day. Be committed to meditation every day. Once you have lengthened your meditation time never reduce it. Always move steadily forward. With discipline and commitment you can achieve anything.

Christine has realized one of the most precious insights mankind can expect to possess, the omnipresence of Creation. In her words...

During commitment weekend in October 1995 I had my most profound meditation.

It was still early in the day and I was meditating on the bluff overlooking the Niangua River. I wanted to know God, truly deep down experience the stillness and love I imagined that would connect me with the Creator.

I was calm, centered and focused. I saw a brilliant light that grew and grew and enveloped me. I stayed there for a long time.

Moments after the meditation ended as I walked down the lane I realized that silence was all around me all the time. So it is everywhere I go. I can hear the silence whenever I want to – all it takes is a still mind.

It is not by chance that Christine's meditation was experienced at the College of Metaphysics campus where the chakra for Intuitive Man, sixth day thinker, is located. Since its inception, the School of Metaphysics World Headquarters has become very spiritualized, and is becoming more and more filled with light every day. The energies here do resonate at a high refined frequency, uplifting the energies of all life forms.

The depth of Christine's meditation experience was influenced by the event at which it occurred – Commitment Weekend. Commitment Weekend at COM is a weekend of fasting, focusing on one's purpose, and meditating intensely with others and with nature. The energies in every way were conducive to the deepest meditation, and many recall remarkable meditations that are as fresh today, in some cases years later, as they were when first experienced.

Christine's discovery during meditation has become an everyday part of her life. Her grasp of spiritual reality was gained much more quickly than normally because of the efforts she had put forth in concentration, meditation, dream interpretation, and through service to others by teaching and healing. She can now recognize and hear the sound of silence anytime, anywhere. She has manifested one of the highest forms of commitment because the omnipresence of Creation is part of her being, part of her life, every moment.

1

I want to cause my meditation to be deeper and deeper every day. What would you suggest?

Meditate every day. Meditate at the same time every day. Meditate in the same peaceful place every day. Have a meditation blanket that you place under you and use each day to separate you from the Earth currents. Develop a deep desire to know yourself. Create a deep desire to know all of creation.

2

Why is it important to meditate every day? Is it really possible to go through a whole day in a meditative state?

The physical body has evolved to function on a day to day basis, sun up to sun up or an approximate 24 hour period. For true progress to occur you must utilize this 24 hour cycle. Activity and rejuvenation and receptivity are all necessary during each 24 hour period in order for progress to be caused.

3

What is meditation?

Meditation is learning to still the mind and listen. This creates a state of receptivity to the inner mind and the Higher Divisions of consciousness throughout your day. Gradually or quickly you will find you are able to take your meditative higher consciousness throughout your day and for all time.

4

How can I create a strong enough purpose or motivation to meditate regularly?

Progress creates motivation. So the first step is to meditate for 15 minutes per day. From this you will begin to see the benefits and your friends will notice the pleasant changes within you. This progress will motivate you to want more and to meditate longer and more deeply.

Read about the benefits others have gained from meditation such as those found in this book. Read about enlightened people throughout history and develop a desire to know what they know.

Ask your teacher about the benefits he or she derives from meditation.

5

What are the benefits of creating a great meditation every day? (Not just aligning my conscious, subconscious, and superconscious minds.) In other words "so what?" This answer is important because I feel that many people including my students start meditation but have difficulty creating a daily deep practice of it.

Peace. A peace and confidence that lets you handle any situation that arises in life with wisdom and success. No longer are you at the mercy of chance or your environment. With meditation you become the director of your life.

No more do you have the wild fluctuations of your emotions. You maintain a peace and equanimity. Your perception becomes much more clear so you know the correct steps to take in any situation. Knowledge and understanding become available to you that previously you were not even aware of.

6

Can meditation help me with my stressful life?

Most definitely. Meditation is a very relaxing, calm and peaceful thing to do. During meditation the muscles of the physical body relax thereby allowing the body to heal and rejuvenate itself. Stress comes from the thoughts of the individual. By stilling the mind in meditation and letting go of the cares and worries of the day, the mind if free to receive awareness from the inner Self which knows only growth, learning, love, and forward motion.

7

What if I don't have time to meditate?

Everyone has time to meditate because everyone has 24 hours in a day. It is a matter of deciding that your soul growth and spiritual awareness, your happiness and joy, your peace and fulfillment, your love and caring, and the well being of your physical, emotional, and mental Self is more important to you than your worries, fears, doubts, limitations, guilt, and problems.

8

Why doesn't everyone meditate?

They have never been taught the value of meditation or a way to meditate. Many people are engrossed or caught up in the physical experience. They have forgotten where they came from and who they are. They have forgotten they are a soul inhabiting a physical body. They are not the physical body.

9

How will I be different if I meditate every day?

You must be committed to meditating every day in order to make rapid progress. From this commitment you will meditate every day and from this you will gain a greater sense of peace and understanding of your purpose in life.

10

What is happening when you feel like you have been pulled down inside yourself? –that is some center part of the head is going to the solar plexus?

This means you need to gain a balance between your inner and outer life. Perhaps you are meditating all day long but never applying it in your life to change, and grow and evolve. It could be that you are not teaching others what you know to be universal truth and what you have discovered in meditation. It also indicates you need to learn to control, direct and use your emotions regularly and wisely.

11

Is it possible to have an enlightening experience in a single meditation that could cause a rapid and quantum change in how fast I accelerate on the spiritual path?

It is possible. The wise man (thinker) uses every experience in their daily life for their permanent and eternal soul growth and spiritual development and to aid others to do the same.

Chapter Five

The Subconscious Mind

When in graduate school at the University of Missouri, I had an unexpected out-of-body experience. It would prove to be the first in a series of spiritual lessons in being more than a physical body and overcoming entrapment in the physical existence.

I had been reading about people who had astrally projected and experienced out of body journeys. I tried a technique given in a book. At the time I was in Peru, South America, working on my Master's thesis. I was in my room one night and had just gone to sleep or was in the process of drifting off into sleep.

All of a sudden I felt a tremendous vibration and a large golden ball of light like a miniature sun come exploding out of my chest with a tremendous *whish.* Immediately after this I found myself on the ceiling of the room looking down at my physical body. I was out of my body! I was astral projecting with conscious awareness! I was excited, thrilled, and amazed but also I experienced fear due to the fact that I had never before, in this lifetime, been consciously separated from my physical body. In a short while my fear brought me back from this unforgettable experience of freedom. I would never be the same again for now I *knew,* without a doubt, that I was not a physical body. I am a soul inhabiting a physical body. The physical body is a vehicle that a person, the soul, gets in at the beginning of a lifetime and rides in or inhabits until the end of a lifetime.

From this point forward my goal became very clear. To overcome the entrapment in a physical body and to live in absolute creative freedom as a soul and as a creator : not to avoid responsibility and not a freedom *from* something but a freedom to grow and expand my consciousness. Freedom to respond to all creation and to humanity's need for soul growth and spiritual development. It wasn't long after this that I entered classes at the Institute known as the School of Metaphysics determined to know myself, my purpose in life, and to know all creation.

About two months later I had the experience with the golden ball of luminescent light once again. This time I had gone to sleep and was in a dream state. In the dream I was lying in a bed in a hotel room. All of a sudden I felt the powerful vibration and then the golden sun-like, luminescent globe of light exploded out of my chest and once again I was out of my body. I was no longer in the dream state but was in an actual out-of-body experience.

Once you have experienced out of body there is no mistaking the difference between imagining being out of the body and actually being out of body. Anyone can daydream about an experience but it requires talent and ability to have that experience.

Dreams are a kind of inner level experience. A projection. A projection of consciousness into the inner levels of mind while an out-of-body experience is a seventh level and a sixth level emotional or etheric experience. One is an outer projection while the other is an inner projection.

By the time I got out of my body the second time I was in an intensive study of dream interpretation and meditation through the School of Metaphysics. This is why this second experience appeared in a dream.

As I progressed in the course work and classes at the Institute I had more expansive consciousness experiences. When audio relaxation tapes, chant tapes, and color tapes were played in class my consciousness would expand to fill the classroom. At other times my mental head would move out of my physical head and I or my mental consciousness would be up on top of the ceiling several feet above my head. This was when I began to see that I could control and direct the expansion of my consciousness.

I began meditating more intensely. After about a year of meditation I could remove my attention from my physical body and still maintain conscious awareness. By this time I had become a teacher in the classes of the School of Metaphysics.

Once during a deep meditation I found myself looking around my room. Then I realized I was still in meditation and my eyelids were closed. In other words I was seeing my room directly with my mind. I was bypassing my physical eyeballs and perceiving directly with my mind. The perception was clear. As clear or more clear than if I was looking with my physical eyes. Then I went back into deep meditation for awhile. After my meditation was completed I slowly brought my attention back to the five senses and physical existence. I noted my experience by writing it down in my journal.

The Subconscious Mind is that division of Mind that most people associate with sleep. At night when the Conscious Mind is shut down and as the person goes to sleep the attention of the individual is transferred to Subconscious Mind. At this time dreaming begins because dreams are communication from the dreamer's subconscious mind to their conscious mind.

The Subconscious Mind, being the older of the two minds, is also the wiser and more knowledgeable of the two minds. A new conscious mind is formed each lifetime as the baby or young child matures into an adult. You do however bring into this life a soul or subconscious mind that has accumulated knowledge and understandings through countless eons.

Just as the physical planet earth contains many different cultures with different languages, so the Subconscious Mind has its own language which is called the Universal Language of Mind. The language of the inner Mind, the Universal Language of Mind is based upon function whereas the language of physical existence is the language of form. This I have discovered in my 35 years of effort to understand the Language of Mind beginning with my early childhood. This was also a process of bringing out my understanding of the Universal Language of Mind stored in my own subconscious mind as part of my permanent memory.

As a person pursues a subject whether it is mathematics, physics, history, or dance, as attention and effort is given to learn and master the subject, not only does the conscious mind learn but the conscious mind is also simultaneously prepared to receive the hidden knowledge and understandings stored as permanent memory in subconscious mind. When you begin the study of a subject and find the learning comes easily or rapidly you can be certain this is a field of study that you have some understanding of, understanding which is stored in your subconscious mind. The duty of the subconscious mind is *to fulfill the desires of the conscious mind.* This it will do if allowed by the conscious mind. This it will accomplish when the conscious mind produces a state of receptivity. Activity toward the desired goal or ideal allows the individual to receive the object of his or her desire into their daily life.

The divisions of Mind are designed to work together in harmony for the growth and maturity of the soul. The Conscious Mind identifying with habits and limitations often refuses to work in harmony with the Subconscious Mind. The Subconscious Mind, however, is always attempting to do what is good and productive for the Conscious Mind, the Subconscious Mind, and the whole Self.

How does the person, while living and operating in the physical day-to-day existence utilizing their conscious mind, develop these Self imposed limitations? The answer is limitations are learned.

Observe a baby. They do not believe it is impossible to walk. They may try to walk one hundred or one thousand times, each time falling down. They never give up, and eventually they do learn to walk. The child never accepts walking as an impossible goal to achieve. They know they will learn to walk because they see adults walking and so they imitate what they observe until what they observe becomes a part of their conscious mind learning.

When a child is taught anger, fear, worthlessness, doubt, or guilt either directly by the parents or indirectly through their thoughts and example then the child will imitate these limitations until they become a part of that child's consciousness and therefore quite real to him or her even if they are imagined limitations. Many of the limitations are learned from adults or older children in the environment. Many people tell children primarily the things they can*not* do instead of encouraging them to imagine *cans* and pursue their dreams.

The only way you will be happy in this lifetime is if and when you pursue your heart's desire, your dream. At some time in everyone's life their heart's desire came to them and their conscious awareness. Most people reject their innermost desire as an impossibility. They think they do not have enough time, energy, or money to achieve their dream. However, the truly successful and fulfilled people are those who have pursued their dreams to the fullest by being totally committed to their ideals and heartfelt desires. These also tend to be, incidentally or not, the people who become happy and monetarily rich.

Since the duty of the Subconscious Mind is to fulfill the desires of the Conscious Mind, what does the Conscious Mind have to give in return?

The answer is *understandings*.

What is it that the Subconscious Mind desires most? The answer is forward motion and evolvement which comes from building permanent memory or permanent understandings. To state it another way, the Subconscious Mind desires understandings to be added to it that can only be produced through growthful change and expansion of consciousness in the Conscious Mind.

The Subconscious Mind fulfills desires of the Conscious Mind enabling the Conscious Mind to build understanding that is then given and stored as permanent memory and learning in Subconscious Mind. The physical brain stores memories of experiences whether imagined or physically experienced. The soul stores permanent memory in the form of understandings.

The Conscious Mind produces and chooses the experiences it will have in order to gain the opportunity to progress, grow, better one's station in life and ultimately produce understanding stored in Subconscious Mind for all eternity. The universal essence of soul in Subconscious Mind is understanding. This is why the soul in Subconscious Mind is aligned with Truth and only presents Truth. The identification of Self is with soul between lifetimes. Therefore, you identify with universal Truth between lifetimes.

Dream communication is a way in which the subconscious mind communicates to the conscious, waking mind of the individual. Through this process the subconscious mind offers valuable knowledge both for the soul progression of the person and for the fulfillment of the desires of the conscious mind.

Just as the subconscious mind reaches the conscious mind in nightly dreams that are remembered, recorded, and interpreted; so the awareness of the person can be trained to reach the subconscious mind.

The training begins with learning to focus the mind with one pointed attention which is called concentration. Concentration, the intentional focusing of the mind on an object or something outside of Self aligns the conscious mind with the subconscious mind. This creates an opportunity and possibility for clear and open communication between the two minds.

In observing the Mind chart *(Diagram 7* on the next page), consider the following.

One of the obvious factors of the mind chart is that it is drawn in the

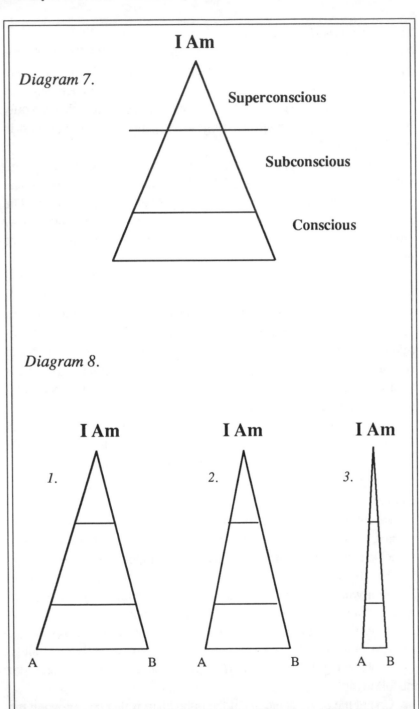

Diagram 7.

I Am

Superconscious

Subconscious

Conscious

Diagram 8.

I Am

1.

A   B

I Am

2.

A   B

I Am

3.

A   B

shape of a triangle. This is not a random feature. The triangular shape symbolizes and indicates the manner in which the attention of the Self in mind becomes more and more scattered and less and less focused the farther removed it is from I AM. This is similar to a flashlight beam that starts out bright but becomes more diffused and dimmer as it moves farther and farther away from its source.

The process of concentration utilized to develop singular attention from a focused and higher directed mind produces a "drawing in effect" on mind that may be illustrated as in *Diagram 8*.

As concentration and the focused mind is utilized and applied in the life of the individual the attention becomes less scattered thereby allowing the Self greater access to all of mind. A person begins to develop a greater sense of oneness with others and a connectedness to family, friends, community, country, and the world. The individual finds he or she can begin to know the thoughts and feelings of others because one's mind can reach out to others as shown in *Example 3*. Instead of experiencing an extreme distance from others as shown illustrated in *Example 1*.

The distance from *Point A* to *Point B* represents the sense of separation you experience the more physically engrossed you are as in *Example 1*. When concentration is practiced the walls of mind come closer together as in *Example 3* and the same experience of distance and separation is reduced or eliminated.

An acorn contains within it the complete idea for the development of a giant oak tree waiting to be called into action by the right environmental conditions and nourishment. Each division of Mind and each level of Mind has a specific duty or idea for the development of the whole Self. The duty of the Conscious Mind is to give permanent understandings to the Subconscious Mind. The duty of the Subconscious Mind is to fulfill the desires and strong mental images of the Conscious Mind.

You truly can create your desires through the proper and productive use of conscious and subconscious minds. A clearly imaged desire, a strong thought form, willfully imaged is planted in the third level of mind, the mental level. The desired thought form will gain mass and substance as it moves through the levels of subconscious mind closer to the physical or seventh level. At last, the desired situation, circumstance, or object will manifest in the thinker's daily life exactly as imaged. This will occur when the desire has been imaged clearly, repeatedly, and the individual has taken action to prepare the Self to receive the object of his or her desire by setting up the physical conditions to receive.

The subconscious mind will work exactly and precisely to fulfill all conscious desires that are clearly and specifically imaged and hardened into substantiality by the action of the will.

When a complete and detailed picture-image of an idea is created in the conscious mind and given to the subconscious mind then the subconscious mind will reach out to anyone with like desires to aid the conscious mind in fulfilling that desire. People with like ideals are drawn together in order that common desires may be fulfilled be they of starting a business or manifesting your divinity.

In our physical existence we experience distance between conscious minds. We experience distance between people. We seem to be separated from others. Life seems to be fragmented. You are in one house and your neighbor is in another house. Unless you walk over to the neighbor's house or telephone that neighbor there is little communication. However, in Universal Subconscious Mind all individual subconscious minds already have a built-in mental, telephone like connection. This connection is built-in as part of the structure of Subconscious Mind. In subconscious existence all subconscious minds are interconnected and have a mental interconnectedness. The telephone is a man made physical invention that somewhat approximates what the Subconscious Mind can and already does achieve. This is also true of most physical inventions.

The television, telescope, and radio are imperfect replications or reproductions of actions the Subconscious Mind already performs. The telephone approximates telepathy while the television imperfectly copies clairvoyance and the radio is a replica of mental broadcasting. All serve to eliminate distance between people.

Meditation is the process of listening and receiving the communication from the inner Self. Communication from the subconscious mind received in meditation may be given in pictures or mental images that is the language of Subconscious Mind. There are times, however, when the subconscious mind may employ words and be direct and to the point because the person has not gone to the effort and joy to learn the Universal Language of Mind. In this case, the inefficient use of words and physical language is the only way in which the subconscious mind can get its message across.

The subconscious mind will go to extreme lengths to fulfill the desires of the conscious mind including but not limited to answering the conscious mind's sincere questions about life, Self, and Creation.

When the sincere student of Mind begins practicing, using, and applying concentration on a daily basis then he or she begins to have awareness of his or her purpose in life. You may look down at your hands after meditation and it will seem as if you have never seen your hands before. It will be as though you are seeing your hands for the first time. You will find them very intriguing and you won't want to stop looking at them. This is because your hands represent your purpose and in the Universal Language of Mind your hands symbolize purpose. When you truly have this experience you will *know* not just believe that you are making great progress in understanding your purpose in life and for this lifetime. I remember when it first happened with me. I had just finished meditating and I looked down at my hands that were placed one over the other in my lap. It seemed as if I were looking at my hands for the first time. It was like I was *seeing* them for the first time. This was because meditation was providing me a way to learn and fulfill my purpose for this lifetime for hands represent purpose. Many years later I read of another person who had the exact same experience with their hands after meditation showing me the universalness of the meditative experience.

When a thought is regularly held in the conscious mind that thought image may be received as communication by the subconscious mind. The language of mind is picture images, that is, mental images. When the mental image created in the conscious mind by the individual is clear and consistent then the inner or subconscious mind receives the message and acts upon it. The subconscious mind goes to work to draw mind substance, the substance of subconscious mind, together around the thought form. This causes an increase in mass and substance of the thought image until gradually, or rapidly, the thought form develops a more substantial form so it can manifest in one's physical life as the creation of the object of our desires. This is the power of the Subconscious Mind; a very powerful secret to be aware of and learn to wield.

An analogy may be drawn between the way a desire or thought moves in Mind to the way rain clouds and rain occurs. When sun shines on the earth, the moisture that has collected in ponds, lakes, rivers, and oceans raises to the sky forming clouds. In a similar fashion when a person creates a clear thought or desire in the conscious, waking mind then shines the light of his attention on that desire it is transferred to the third level of Mind. The third level of Mind is the deepest or most refined level of Subconscious Mind.

Just as a raindrop forms around a speck of dust or gathers moisture around a speck of dust so does a thought form placed in Subconscious Mind begin to draw mind substance around itself. When enough moisture has been collected and conditions are right, the clouds begin to release moisture in the form of rain. The rain falls or moves from the clouds in the sky to the ground below which is analogous to the thought form moving from the third level of Mind through the fourth, fifth, sixth levels of Mind until it finally reaches the seventh level of Consciousness, the physical existence.

All that has been created in our physical existence was first impressed as a seed idea in the third level of its creator's Consciousness. As the seed idea moves through the third and fourth levels of Consciousness, it draws around itself mind substance, becoming heavier and gaining in mass or substance.

In the fourth level of Mind, your subconscious mind reaches out to all other minds to aid you in fulfilling the object of your desire. Fully manifesting productive desires is a step or stage of learning the process of creation. You can use this to cause rapid soul growth and spiritual transformation within Self.

Similarly a thought form clearly created in the conscious mind through the use of directed imaging and held firm and consistent with the will gives the subconscious mind an image to act on. It also gives an opportunity for Mind substance to be drawn to and collect around the thought form. The seed idea can begin to grow and mature into a fully developed form much as an acorn becomes an oak tree.

In the fifth level of Mind, ideas begin to take on physical attributes. The object of one's desires begins to receive substance in the third level of mind, then fourth level. By the time the thought form has reached the fifth level, the thought form has assumed a form more closely resembling the initial image. In the fifth level of Mind the beginning of separation of vibration occurs such as male and female, the colors such as green, red, yellow, and hot and cold. At the fifth level of consciousness the separation of the thought form into various aspects begins. Instead of a connectedness with everything the individual begins to experience separation. This is the point of the beginning of the separation between heat and cold.

In the fourth level of consciousness ideas begin to take on individuality. Within the fourth level of Mind ideas begin an expansive process.

The third level of consciousness is the place in Mind where thoughts begin to gain substance in order that later they may manifest in our daily lives as the object of our desires. Each desire begins in the physical existence when the environmental stimulus re-acts and impinges on one or more of the five senses. You see or smell food and subsequently you desire food. You see a person of the opposite sex, and you are attracted to that person. You see and feel soft or fancy clothes and you want those clothes. As the conscious mind formulates a desire and the individual holds their conscious attention on the desire until the image is clearly formulated then the image can be sent from the conscious or seventh level of Mind to the third or deepest level of the Subconscious Mind.

The level of Mind closest to the physical level of consciousness is the Emotional level of consciousness. An analogy for the manner in which the emotional level of Mind interacts with the seventh level or Conscious Mind is honey and the honeycomb. The honeycomb is analogous to the physical level and Conscious Mind while the honey fills the honeycomb may be likened to Emotional level of Mind.

The sixth or Emotional level of Mind appears to be the opposite of the physical in many respects. An analogy may be drawn between a photograph and the negative of the photograph held on the film. In case of the negative film everything appears to be in reverse of the physical. For example black is white and right is left. Red will appear green and blue will appear orange.

The emotions need to be understood and utilized daily in the outer, physical life as a part of one's creation in order to learn how to go deeper into Mind than the sixth level of consciousness.

These inner levels are the domain of the soul. One student's experience brings all of these elements together very well. A self-employed transcriptionist and stenographer, Karen's meditation occurred during a day of meditation proclaimed annually by the School of Metaphysics as the best way we know how to "make a difference."

*On Make A Difference Day (an annual call for
volunteerism sponsored by USA Today Newspaper and other
national corporations), October 26, 1996, I had probably my
most profound meditation experience to date. We set aside an
entire 24-hour period where we ate sparingly, slept little, and
kept our thoughts and conversations focused on God and on
world peace. I believe this is one of the few times in my life I
have truly experienced a Sabbath Day.*

*About halfway through the day, I sat in the chapel listening
to the fountain and the chanting of the Eternal Om, preparing
to meditate. As my mind stilled, in my mind's eye I saw a cave.
It was a long cave with a cathedral-like ceiling. I was a man
seated in a circle of 100 men. As I listened to the fountain, I
looked across at the cave wall and saw rivulets of water
cascading down the rock wall. The water formed a clear, cool
pool in a natural rock basin that we sometimes drank from.*

*As I listened to the chanting of the Om, I remembered how
our voices echoed through the cave, and we chanted softly, so
that the echo would not be thunderous. The cave was in the
high mountains of Tibet.*

*I finally recognized this place as the cave I had been led to
by my spirit guide during my meditation at Wesak. Wesak
occurs when the sun is in Taurus, and the moon is in Scorpio.
This is a gathering of disincarned and incarned entities, who
are interested in the spiritual evolution of the humanity. In my
Wesak experience, I was there but seconds, and I was quickly
jerked out of my experience by my fear. I saw a circle of light
beings in a great cave. I could make out no features, they were
just beings of light.*

*When I meditated again, I again saw this place with a
circle of 100 men. I asked why I had been given this information. I was told that my soul was among a group of souls
whose mission was to raise the vibration of humanity, and to
aid in ushering in the time of spiritual intuitive man.*

*This really came as no surprise to me, since that is what
my activities in the School of Metaphysics are geared toward.
This is the purpose of the School of Metaphysics, which we say*

in the opening projection of our classes. I remember the first
time I heard those words in the opening projection. I was filled
with many emotions all at once, surprise that the teacher had
added these words to the opening projection used previously,
excitement that this was the School of Metaphysics' purpose,
and recognition of the fact that I was in the right place to
pursue my learning and growth.

Although this information was not new to me, I was taken
aback by having it reinforced so vividly in my meditation. This
was clearly being stated as my soul's purpose. I am still filled
with several emotions, awe that I received this insight and of
course disbelief and the thought that my ego made this up, and
trepidation regarding what I see as an awesome responsibility.
There is also a sense of elation of knowing my soul's purpose,
and that I am on the right track.

This rich and rewarding meditation experience that Karen had was the result of her own efforts in meditation leading up to the repeated and prolonged meditations of this Day of Meditation. Devotion and dedication prepare the Self for deeper and deeper realizations that enlighten the spirit, mind, and body. Karen's connection with her soul's purpose was also the result of spending the whole weekend in this serene setting, focusing on nothing other than her soul growth and Self understanding.

Karen's experience was also the result of meditating with others of like mind some of whom had been meditating much longer than she. We are indeed all connected, and of this Karen is assured. Having experienced psychic happenings all her life Karen knew about feelings and impressions and the many subtle ways people influence one another. What she has learned by developing her intuitive powers has enabled her to expand her understanding and practice. Meditation has uplifted her. And since this meditation experience she now knows how her thoughts affect others and how others' thoughts affect her for the greater good of all.

1

What is the Subconscious Mind?

The home or abode of the soul.

2

Where is Subconscious Mind?

Everywhere.

3

Why can't we see it?

The conscious mind is designed to work with or function through the five senses of sight, hearing, smell, taste, and touch, the Subconscious Mind is not. The Subconscious Mind vibrates at a higher rate or frequency than the five senses can detect.

4

What is the duty of the Subconscious Mind?

To fulfill desires of the conscious mind.

5

What is the purpose of the Subconscious Mind?

To store permanent understandings.

6

What is the emotional or sixth level of mind or consciousness?

The outpush or expression of energy as it moves from the Subconscious Mind to the Conscious Mind.

7

What is the fifth level or lower astral level of consciousness?

The place in Mind where energy begins to coalesce or contract as form.

8

What is the fourth level of consciousness?

The place in which the thought or desire connects with similar thought forms.

9

What is the third level of consciousness?

The origination point of thought.

10

What is Universal Mind?

Universal Mind is the quality of the Subconscious Mind that allows mind to mind connection between individuals at distances beyond what is possible with the five senses. In the Subconscious Mind we have a universal connection with everyone else.

Subconscious Meditation

Once the body and mind are stilled and quieted the attention of the meditator is free to receive from the Subconscious Mind. The very act of stilling the conscious mind causes there to be an alignment of the conscious and subconscious minds of the meditator.

When you have achieved this state you may begin to experience things you never have before. After I had been meditating for several months I had the following experience. Sometimes toward the end of the meditation period I noticed I could see everything in the room in which I was meditating without turning my head. I realized that my eyelids were completely closed. I was seeing or perceiving with my Subconscious Mind the actual physical surroundings. I became very excited about this.

My students have reported seeing colored lights, having visions or hearing words in answer to their prayers or petitions. The answers seemed almost like someone was in the room saying them aloud.

Whatever you experience as your meditation deepens into subconscious mind it is important to always focus on receiving the answer to your question and to expectantly listen for that answer. When the meditation time is completed you can write down your experiences, if you so desire.

The surest sign you are making progress in meditation is the deepening peace you experience during and after each meditation. The alignment of the inner and outer minds, the conscious and subconscious mind, produces this peace.

Instead of a battle to discipline your conscious mind and physical body you now experience peace and pleasure from the time you begin your meditation to the time you finish and beyond. In fact, this peace that "passeth all understanding" you carry with you throughout the day. Most people are wanting greater peace and less chaos and less reactions in their life. Meditation becomes a way of life and the peace you gain in meditation becomes a part of your life. In fact, peace becomes more and more your life.

When Pamela was in her early forties, the depth of her meditations became pronounced. This was following a significant connection experienced during a daily meditation time, a connection that has continued, and strengthened, since that time.

In the advanced lessons of the School of Metaphysics, I reached the point where I was ready to begin perceiving, understanding, and using Heart chakra energies. During this time I was meditating and heard a voice which said, "I've been waiting for you." The voice was like that of a long lost loved one who had been missing me for a long time. Now finally we were reunited. The feeling I experienced from that voice was one of profound peace and love like someone who had returned to the comfort and security of home after a long separation. I knew this was my inner Self speaking and tears welled up in my eyes.

The School of Metaphysics gives instruction in the use of the Heart chakra as a point of meditation. This is an advanced spiritual discipline. The quality of the heart chakra is love and understanding. The voice that Pamela heard was her own Subconscious mind, her soul, her soulmate which is the conscious mind's soulmate.

From the time each individual incarns in a physical body they begin to move their attention away from their inner love, their subconscious mind, their soul, their soulmate. From the time of incarnation in a baby's body your soul is waiting for you, engrossed in the conscious mind and physical body, to move out of your entrapment and turn inward. Your soul, which is you, awaits the time when the disciplined, meditative, conscious mind will achieve contact once again with the soul. Through meditation the conscious mind and subconscious mind of the individual are aligned. This is the marriage made in heaven. This is when you live in the world but are not of it.

When the conscious awareness is re-united with the subconscious mind you may live and operate from a subconscious or soul perspective while going through your physical actions. Your physical life takes on a whole new meaning for you. Actions you were previously doing are now done with a totally new intention and purpose.

The profound peace and love experienced comes from the alignment of the mind. Pam was moving closer to God and the source of all creation. At the source of all creation is peace and love. It is only here in the physical experience that we experience discord, strife, confusion, and refusal to remember where you came from.

Your inner Self and the inner Mind is where your true home is. It is where you came from.   Each person's true security and comfort come from their true home which is the inner Mind, more specifically, the Superconscious Mind.

The inner Self, the Real Self, is always endeavoring to contact and communicate with the engrossed soul existing in a physical body. The tears are from the profound sense of joy and happiness that comes from knowing the inner, Real Self.

Perception heightens as more of the mind is used. Perception, or the combining of the five senses of taste, touch, smell, sound, and sight through concentration, produces a sixth sense called perception. Perception is the ability to perceive directly with the mind. Perception extends beyond what is normally available to the five senses. The abilities of clairvoyance, clairaudience, telepathy, and other so-called "psychic" abilities are factors of the Subconscious Mind and are sometimes experienced by the meditator who has disciplined, stilled, and focused the mind.

When these perceptions and abilities manifest or appear in your life take note of them realizing they are not the ultimate goal you are seeking in meditation. They are experiences designed to stimulate you and motivate you on to higher and deeper levels of meditation so you progress on from Subconscious meditation to Superconscious meditation.

Meditation enables the individual to learn more from each experience. Meditation gives the meditator the capacity to intentionally and willfully create and build permanent understanding at a greatly accelerated rate. Meditation makes it possible for the Self to rapidly integrate the knowledge gained from experiences into the Self to form understandings. In this way as meditation deepens the meditator may increase his rate of soul growth 10 fold, 100 fold, or even 1000 fold and more!

In this meditation your consciousness expands into Subconscious Mind. You are able to concentrate and focus the attention. You are also able to remove your attention form the physical body thus freeing the attention from the conscious mind and physical part of Self.

Meditation by this time has become a peaceful and very pleasant experience. It is no longer an effort or fight to sit still in one place for 15 minutes or even an hour for you have gained a certain degree of mastery over your physical body. You and your physical body enjoy sitting still for meditation. It has become a very relaxing and pleasant experience. You enjoy the fact that your muscles relax and your body receives rest and rejuvenation during meditation. Meditation has been an important and necessary part of your life and you crave it. Instead of looking at meditation as something you have to force yourself to do, meditation has become a joyous pleasure that is the highlight of your day.

At first it seemed difficult to make time for meditation but now twenty-year-old Lisa is discovering daily meditation is a must, the perfect complement to her hectic college and work schedule. It gives her perspective and freedom of thought that otherwise would be lacking in her life.

> *Actually the best meditation I have had was really perfect. I felt myself rising up through the clouds. I went through the clouds and it was dark and still. I looked around. I was waiting for God to show up. I was very peaceful. I had zero attention on my physical body. Everything was so open and expansive. It was warm like love is and there was a light even in the darkness/stillness. When I came out I was surprised how long I had been in.*

Three common qualities of experience that people have when they attain a closeness to God in meditation are extreme sense of peace, an all encompassing love, and or a very bright, and brilliant white or golden light.

Rising up and above the clouds is representative of directing or moving one's consciousness higher and higher to the highest levels of mind. Lisa mentions here that she had zero attention on her physical body at this time. It is necessary to remove your attention from the physical body in order to go deep in meditation and scale the heights necessary to know I AM and have superconscious awareness.

Light, love, and peace all are present as a part of this meditation. All indicate a successful meditation and that the meditator is making rapid progress in her soul growth and spiritual awareness.

When the attention is removed from the physical body the mind ceases to register physical time as much. Thus, one can engage in meditation for a long period of time in this state and when you come out of it it seems as if only a short time has passed. Time in subconscious mind is measured by the understandings you build while time in the physical existence is measured by a sequence of events such as sunrise to sunrise.

During and after meditation you notice a gentle peace has settled over your entire being. All stress is gone. You feel more attuned to the Creator and Creation. When you open your eyes after meditation you notice everything is lighter and brighter.

You notice the vertebrae of your spine slip into place because your muscles are so relaxed and all tension and stress is gone. You find your days go much more smoothly and with less conflict than before you started meditating. You find yourself re-acting to life much less. You are responding to your inner desires much more easily and quickly. Your life is more fulfilling.

You discover that your purpose in life has become much more clear. You know that life has meaning and you have a unique assignment for this lifetime. You begin to realize that you have something valuable to offer to humanity. Therefore, your life takes on more meaning, worth, and value. You realize you are not just living your life for you alone but are, in fact, living your life for many more people. You realize your importance in the scheme of things. Your conception and understanding of who you are grows and understands.

You begin to understand that you have a universal connection with everyone and you desire to serve humanity and to aid others in their soul growth and teach others how to quicken their inner life and spiritual development.

You may develop *extra*sensory perception for your perception does reach a heightened level and your awareness and intuitive faculties grow. Students often speak of inner level communication with their infant children, distant relatives, and loved ones who have departed physical existence. The heightened sense of connection has its very practical expression in our relations with others. Spiritual disciplines hone the mind to experience the freedom of experiencing in the inner levels.

Subconscious meditation increases one's ability to perceive with subconscious mind and thereby have higher perception. These higher perceptions may include clairaudience, the ability to hear at extremely long distances, clairvoyance, the ability to see or perceive at a distance far beyond what the eyes alone could perceive, or telepathy, the ability to communicate mentally with others over long distances. All or any of these may increase and more.

However, none of these extra-sensory abilities are your goal. Your ultimate goal is enlightenment. Your ultimate goal is to know and to be one with the Creator while at the same time maintaining your individuality and identity as a Creator in your own right. Then you become a son of the Supreme Creator.

Signs you are making progress in Meditation

1. Twenty minutes in meditation stops seeming like it is a long time, a long length of time. Instead, you ask yourself is 20 minutes up already? It seems like I just got started a couple of minutes ago.

2. You become very relaxed.

3. You may experience a tingling sensation throughout your body during or at the end of meditation. This is due to this nervous system being stimulated and revivified by the energies of the Higher levels of Mind and consciousness that are moving into your Being.

4. A sense of peace coming over and within you.

5. A buzzing or tingling in the head signaling a higher Consciousness.

By the time you have reached Subconscious meditation the physical body is no longer fighting against you, the thinker. Instead the body has been disciplined and brought under your command and is willing to do your bidding. Your physical body as your willing servant remains still and at peace during meditation. There are no bodily itches distracting you from your meditation for you do not even notice your body during meditation.

Preparation for meditation is easy because you have laid the foundation with your conscious mind meditation. You are able to concentrate and focus your mind. You are able to remove your attention from your body. You know how to present your petition or prayer in meditation.

You are committed to your meditation. You meditate at least once a day for at least a half an hour. Probably you are meditating at least forty five minutes to an hour each day. You may even be meditating twice a day, once in the morning and again in the evening before going to bed.

At this time you may begin chanting the AUM vibration or sound. Be sure to enunciate all three letters out loud. AUM is the vibration of Creation. By chanting or sounding the word AUM you are aligning your consciousness with the Creator's consciousness. You are aligning your vibration with the vibration of Creation. When you say the word AUM prior to your meditation stretch the word out. Make it last for several seconds so the vibration infiltrates your entire being.

Debbie, a mature woman who is just beginning to meditate, describes an experience which accurately reflects the openness, the wonder, the innocence of infancy and the need for wise counsel while learning.

> *I was larger than myself. I could see the whole room. A man was standing near me.*
>
> *After singing the AUM chant I heard a loud tone in the room. It was a very loud tone. I opened my eyes and turned my head to the left and then to the right. It was still there in the room.*
>
> *I felt a vibration in the note of "FA". I closed my eyes and tried to relax the sound. Everything else was quiet, the room was quiet. I did keep thinking, "Boy this sure is distracting to my meditation." Later after asking my teacher, she said I should listen to the sound.*

Meditation creates an expansion of consciousness that enables one to see or perceive all around the room, all sides of the room simultaneously as if one had eyes in the back of their head. You can see all around you, the full 360 all at one time. Unlike the physical eyes, consciousness and perception have no limitations except those the person places on himself. The cosmic sound AUM is the vibration of creation. It is the vibration that the Universe vibrates or moves to. It is the vibration of energy that the universe uses to create. When you meditate you will learn to hear sounds you have never heard before as you go beyond the physical sense of hearing and learn to hear with the mind.

When meditation is repeated with full attention and expanded intention, the cumulative effect is progressively enlightened awareness of space, time, and Self. The messages received from the inner levels of consciousness become more poignant.

> *My best meditation ever was Commitment weekend. It was a beautiful fall day with wind gently blowing. The surroundings of nature were so calming and quiet. I could smell the soil and grass and the trees waved so slightly.*
>
> *There were a series of six meditation stations available for us. At first I had a hard time staying focused. My senses distracted me, I was hungry. All I could think of was what I had done earlier and what I needed to accomplish later. My thoughts of my desires were a distraction.*
>
> *Each meditation throughout the day became deeper by the time I was at my fifth meditation spot and experiencing greater calmness and clarity of mind I received this message. "Once a foundation of peace is built then bliss is experienced throughout the whole being."*
>
> *Then I experienced a shower of love tingles as if I was a sparkler lit. There was a body of light being birthed it reminded me of the birth of Jesus. I experienced moving inward, gaseous clouds, expansiveness, contraction, a picture of a vehicle like Star Trek much cruder in physical appearance. There was control and command of holding my attention still.*
>
> *I was so peaceful and calm. I could meditate for hours.*

Commitment weekend is an event held on the College of Metaphysics campus every other year in the fall. The campus is huge. It contains over 1500 acres of land with trees, hills, valleys, and beauty all around. The participants spend all day meditating at these different beautiful places in nature and writing down their wonderful and new awarenesses.

During his meditation, Ernie received the truth that, "Once a foundation of peace is built then bliss is experienced throughout the whole being." The foundation of peace is built by stilling the mind and disciplining the physical body to remain still. Peace comes from a still mind and a life that is focused on service to one's High Self and service to mankind. Bliss is the experience of the alignment of all minds.

The shower of love tingles occurred because Ernie delved deep into the understanding of Creation and discovered that it is impregnated, infused, and saturated with Love. Love draws us to know LIGHT. LOVE gives us the burning desire and need to know our true essence which is LIGHT.

Again we see there was control and command of the attention and a still mind. This led to knowing LOVE and LIGHT.

Perhaps the most rewarding part of this meditation is that in the end, Ernie was very peaceful. In fact, peace is the surest sign you are making progress in meditation. When you experience peace in meditation or immediately after meditation you can be sure you are making progress. Even if you do not have any visions for a long time after learning to meditate you will still know you are making progress when the peace you experience continues to deepen. At times you may gain such a sense of peace in meditation that you will want to continue it on for a longer time period. Conflict is a function of our physical experience it is not part of the true deepest levels of the inner mind. When you experience peace you experience your true, High Self which is the Real Self.

Ernie's progressive meditation also mentions being birthed in a body of light. Light is our essence and when you identify with the inner Self through meditation you are closer to the source of our being and closer to the light of the Creator.

This meditation occurred at Commitment Weekend when many others were meditating and when he was in a quiet environment of nature. Both of these factors are conducive to meditation and helped Ernie enhance his meditation experience. It is on a small scale a glimpse of what the world can be as more and more of the individuals on the planet raise their consciousness through daily meditation upon their Creator.

1

What is meditation?

Meditation is the science and art of aligning the outer Self or conscious mind with the inner Self, the subconscious mind. Then with time and practice attuning both conscious and subconscious minds to the superconscious mind.

2

Why does a person want to or need to meditate?

Meditation feels good. The experiences you have in meditation can be the most rewarding and peaceful experiences you will ever have. Meditation makes possible greater fulfillment and happiness in your life.

3

How can meditation benefit me in the long run?

By meditating regularly and consistently you will gain greater direction in your life and you will discover your true purpose. You will become more productive and efficient in everything you do. You will be a better friend and draw to you the greatest friendships you have ever had. You will deepen your understanding and experience of love.

4

When was meditation invented?

Meditation was invented when people were created as a way for each person to know the inner, real Self and to reach their full potential and to know all of creation.

5

Are prayer and meditation the same thing?

No. They are two halves to a whole action of the mind. Prayer is the aggressive act of stating your desire to the inner Self while meditation begins with stilling the conscious mind in order to receive the answers to your prayers from first your soul and later from Superconscious Mind.

6

Is it possible to learn to love to meditate?

Yes. Individuals throughout history and today have learned to love to meditate. Anyone who meditates regularly and consistently will over time or quickly learn to love to meditate.

7

Will meditation help me to find my soul mate?

Most definitely.

8

Can meditation go deeper than the Subconscious Mind?

Yes. As meditation deepens from practice, effort, understanding; then over time the meditator enters Superconscious Mind.

9

What happens when I get good at meditation?

All inner desires arc fulfilled. You gain peace that surpasses all understanding. Your body becomes full of light. You understand the purpose of life. You become a creator. All this and more.

10

What is the difference between an individual's subconscious mind and the Subconscious Mind?

Each person has a conscious mind they use in the division of mind referred to as Conscious Mind which we call the physical experience. Each individual has a subconscious mind which exists as soul in the Universal or Subconscious Mind.

11

What is the difference between the Subconscious Mind and the unconscious?

The Subconscious Mind is where the soul, the eternal part of us resides. The unconscious is a part of the physical brain. The unconscious is memory images stored in the brain often without conscious awareness that the individual does not understand and therefore, still re-acts to with fear, doubts, angers, resentments, guilts, and so forth.

Chapter Six

Emotions

The emotions are the "glue" that binds the Conscious Mind to the Subconscious Mind. The emotional level of Mind is the part of the Subconscious Mind that exists closest to and borders on the Conscious Mind and the physical existence.

The emotions are the way your thought forms are moved or pushed by you from Subconscious Mind into physical existence. The emotions are the expression of energy as it moves from the Subconscious to the Conscious Mind. Charismatic people are able to direct their emotions outward through their words and actions. They are able to move us, excite us, and stimulate us with their oratory and moving speeches.

Without the emotional level of mind you would have no way of moving your thoughts, creations, inventions, and desires from an idea to an outwardly manifested part of your life. Without the emotional level of mind you would have no way of creating the object of your desire. The value of manifesting physical objects as a part of your life is in learning to create and thereby become more like and more compatible to our Creator. A thinker, a reasoner, learns quickly that physical objects and physical possessions in and of themselves do not give enlightenment nor do they grant peace, contentment, or true happiness. They may, and sometimes do, provide a temporary stimulus to the conscious mind but that stimulus is always temporary. This is because the very essence of physical existence is temporary.

Emotion is the energy to move one's thoughts from a mental concept or construct into a physical manifestation. The secret of life is: a complete idea becoming a physical manifestation that is a creation or object in our lives. The proper use of the emotions enables this manifestation part of the creation process to occur much more rapidly and easily.

Some people mistakenly think they have more control of their life when they keep their thoughts and emotions or feelings to themselves. The truth is that control is not created by repression, confining, holding back or restriction. Control is built by acting on your ideals with purpose, and by teaching and giving service to others.

Meditation is a process of opening up as well as being a process of going within. Yes, your consciousness will go within into the inner levels of Mind in meditation as your meditation deepens over time. It is also true that meditation will expand your consciousness to fill or encompass all of Mind. Part of this expansion is the opening up of the Self. Since the emotional level or sixth level of Mind is the level closest to our physical existence the emotions are a part of ourselves that we must come to understand and utilize wisely early on.

You need to appreciate the wide range of emotions that exist. Most people allow their emotions to use them rather than directing their emotions productively. They constantly re-act emotionally in the same way with the same few restricted emotions. There is a whole range and variety of emotions that are a part of Self and need to be a part of one's expression. All can be useful to aid the Self in becoming aware of the thoughts of Self and also in touching others with your influence.

Sympathy is taking on the difficulties of others. Empathy is the direct perception and understanding of someone else's experience. Make empathy an understanding of Self.

For every idea that moves into physical manifestation there are hundreds that never become more than an idea. What moves this thought form from an idea to a physical manifestation? The answer is emotion.

Gregg, a twenty-two year old computer drafter, was grappling with the emotional push that was enabling his life to begin to unfold as he entered adulthood.

> *My greatest meditation came at a time when I was moving quickly toward fulfilling my desires. I just gained a managerial position, I was beginning a new relationship and I was in a state of Self acceptance.*
>
> *My experience was like a flip into subconscious mind. I say flip because I felt as though I was doing a back flip. I didn't know which end was up. Then I felt as though I was in*

the center of a sphere, a very bright colorful sphere. Then I
had a perspective of objectiveness over my whole life. I began
to know that everything would eventually be okay. It was a
feeling of total confidence that whatever happens, everything
would eventually work out.

The bright, colorful sphere that Greg experienced is the sphere of his own awareness. The bright, or light indicates awareness. As one's consciousness expands one's sphere of influence expands and one's sphere of awareness expands also. As the meditator's consciousness grows beyond the narrow confines of limited thinking he finds that he can view his earlier life or the earlier parts of his life with the objectivity of a person who is no longer involved or engrossed. Just as you can read of someone else's experience and view it objectively, so you will learn to see your whole life objectively as you rise above and beyond your previous limitations.

From the practice of meditation the meditator removes the shackles and limitations of engrossed thinking. The old emotional attachments to people, places and things cease to bind the Self. In their place one develops true love and caring that does not try to control or limit others or Self.

The total confidence came from the fact that Greg had reached a state of objectivity with himself and his life. As he continues to meditate, using this awareness in his life, the objectivity and expansion of consciousness can become a permanent part of himself.

All thoughts are real and have reality. Thought is cause and your thoughts affect the whole planet Earth and everyone on it. You are not separate and apart from all creation. Rather the Self that is you is connected with all other people, entities, and individuals. Everything you do affects every other part of creation. By admitting and claiming authority and responsibility for your life you admit you cause and have caused your life to be as it is. Therefore, since you have caused your life to be as it is up to this point, you can cause it to be different in the future. A higher deity or outside force is not controlling you. The truth is that a higher deity has given you creativity and you are responsible for using your creativity to better yourself.

There are three parts to any and all creations.

1. *Mental*
2. *Emotional*
3. *Physical*

There is a reciprocal action that occurs between the Subconscious Mind and the Conscious Mind or physical existence, in the manifestation of any desire, idea, invention, or creation. This reciprocal action is dependent upon the emotions and the Emotional level of Mind.

Emotions and the Loop

When a thought form is in the process of manifestation it moves through the levels of Subconscious Mind until it moves into the Emotional or sixth level of Mind which is the level of Mind adjacent to the physical; the Conscious level of Mind.

Prior to manifesting into the physical existence from the sixth level of Mind the thought form begins to manifest outward. Indications that one's mental desire-thought form-creation is about to manifest into the physical begins to occur. This means your thought form is about to appear or become a part of your outward, waking, daily life.

You may find yourself in a state of euphoria as you begin to realize more and more that you are about to manifest the object of your desire. You may receive some money or opportunity to make more money or gain wealth that you were not even consciously aware of. When these opportunities present themselves from sources that you had not considered you may be aware that the object of your desire, your visualized thought form-image, is moving closer to manifestation. Your heartfelt desire only awaits your receptivity and preparedness in order to manifest.

At this time, examine your life and state of affairs to discern if you are ready to receive the object of your desire into your daily life. This may entail some changes in your life and in giving up your old, worn out, limitations, and/or habits.

This action just described is called the *loop*. The way the thought form begins to impinge on the physical and move into one's life is an indication of impending success. This movement into the emotional or sixth level of Mind and the pressure on the seventh level of Mind or the Conscious Mind from the emotional level is a preparation for the final, total, great push as an outward part of one's daily life. It is the opportunity for the thought form to gain substance, form, strength, and solidity.

Most people experience emotion only as re-action. Someone does something you don't like so you re-act with anger. Somebody does some thing you like so you re-act with temporary happiness. Observe a child. When she gets the candy she wants she is happy until the candy is gone. Do not let her have the candy she wants and she is angry and may cry. This is the way most adults experience life. They are happy when they get the physical things they want and unhappy, sad, or angry when they do not get the things they want.

Your wants are many, your needs are few. Your wants or desires are almost limitless. You can never fulfill all your desires for by their very nature desires are temporary. Put a piece of candy in your mouth and suck on it. The combination of sweetness and flavor taste good. Soon the candy is gone and you no longer have the sweetness in your mouth so you want another piece of candy, and another, and another. You also notice the second piece of candy does not taste quite as good as the first. The third piece of candy does not taste quite as good as the second piece. Soon, you are feeling ill from a sugar overdose. So you have reached a state of diminishing returns but your desires or sensory engrossment are still controlling you.

Another example of the temporary sensory gratification of desire or wants is buying clothes. You can go out and buy a new shirt or dress every day all the time thinking, "how pretty this is" and yet tomorrow you want a new shirt or dress because the temporary joy of the newness has worn off.

The proper use of desires for physical desired objects or things is to provide food, shelter, and clothing to take care of your physical body's needs so that the soul inhabiting the body can have the opportunity to fulfill the assignment it chose for this lifetime.

Most people re-act to emotions. They either avoid or ignore their emotions and the emotions of others. Have you ever seen a person begin crying in front of a bunch of people. For example, when they are all sitting at a table. When the person begins sobbing most people don't know what to do with the emotional energy being given off. They either sit there in their seats very uncomfortably or they try to hug the person or they interrupt the person by asking what is wrong. Rarely do they use the emotional experience for their soul growth and spiritual development.

I have discovered that when a person is in an out of control emotional state that I can breathe in that other person's emotions. Instead of fighting against their emotions by trying to throw up mental and emotional walls around myself, I direct my mind to totally receive the other person's emotions and totally transform the emotional energy into a higher form of energy. Then I am free to use this higher, transformed, energy for my purposes of quickening my and others' soul growth and spiritual energies. In this way the energy is neither misused or wasted.

When you erroneously believe you have to erect emotional or mental walls around yourself you are wasting most of your mental, emotional, or spiritual energy on merely protecting yourself. This leaves little or no mental energy for soul growth and spiritual development and so the Self stagnates.

By breathing in other people's emotions you are able to focus your attention while completely receiving into yourself what it is the other person is experiencing. Thereby, you are able to empathize with rather than sympathizing with them or rejecting them by putting up mental and emotional walls of protection. To sympathize is to lose your own Self in the other person's problems. The thinker causes the physical desires to evolve to mental and spiritual desires for soul growth and spiritual development. As your desires evolve you operate more and more from the standpoint of real inner needs that come from your inner soul urge. The more you meditate the more you come in contact with, are aware of, and make decisions based upon this inner soul urge. Then you find and gain true, lasting, and permanent happiness, because you are doing what you are supposed to be doing this lifetime. You are fulfilling your purpose and assignment for this lifetime.

When people re-act with their emotions due as they see it to not getting what they want or out of fear of being exposed and found wanting; at those times I breathe in other people's emotions. Have you ever noticed how uncomfortable people get when someone is re-acting either by crying or sadness. Most people erect mental walls around themselves when someone is re-acting near them in an attempt to block the other person's pain from coming into them. It is a protective re-action.

I do just the opposite. I breathe other person's emotions into myself. Then having fully received the other person's emotion I assimilate it and understand it rather than running from it. No learning or understanding is gained from running away from that which seems to be uncomfortable or unpleasant. In fact, people who avoid certain situations because they are uncomfortable are usually people who are stagnant and refuse to change, grow, and learn. Having received the emotions of the other person I transmute the emotional energy into a higher vibration of healing energy. Next I offer the transmitted healing energy back to the hurting person for their overall healing and general benefit.

In this way I aid the other person to move through the problem quicker and evolve to a higher state of consciousness where they no longer feel the need to protect themselves.

Most everyone needs to learn to be more receptive. The method I have just given enables you in any situation to focus your mind and attention on being more receptive. Thereby, you will be able to receive much more of the experience and learning that your environment and the people in it provide you.

Giving thanks also is a very good way to enhance and create receptivity.

Meditation and the Emotions

When a person starts meditation there is a need to concentrate, focus, and still the mind. This requires some degree of effort. For many years you have allowed your thoughts to wander. If you are 20 years old, you probably have allowed your thoughts to wander for 20 years. If you are 50 years old, you have probably allowed your thoughts and attention to wander for 50 years. Therefore, a few weeks or months of effort to correct these years of having an undisciplined mind are well worth the effort.

When you sit down to meditate your undisciplined mind will tend to run to mental images of your past. In other words those images previously stored in the brain will surface. When you sit down in the cross-legged meditation position and close your eyes in a quiet room or place you will notice there are very little external stimuli. Since there are little external stimuli during meditation the conscious ego begins to search for stimuli. It searches the brain for mental images that will provoke a response or re-action. This re-action then leads to the swelling of emotions. The next thing you know you are all involved in anger, resentment, fear, desire, or sadness rather than receiving the glory of LIGHT from the eternal.

Emotional re-actions keep you earthbound. They keep you bound physically to memories of physical experiences in the past. Your true desire is to transcend the physical existence and move your consciousness deep into Subconscious and from there to Superconscious Mind.

Therefore, train your attention as you would train an animal. When you tell your attention to stay you expect your attention to stay in one spot until you say different. Control your thoughts and you control your emotions. Still your mind and you quiet and still your emotions. Then the emotions no longer distract you.

Emotions are not the cause of anything. Emotions are a re-action to your thought. *Your* thoughts are the cause of *your* emotions. Change the thought and the change in emotions follow.

In addition, share your enthusiasm, joy, delight, bliss, and happiness with others. As you open up during your daytime, waking hours you will find the energy flows freely from the inner Subconscious Mind to the outer or Conscious Mind and physical existence. Because of this process of free movement of energy you will no longer find yourself trying to sort through unused and misdirected emotional energy during meditation.

Your meditation is to be a time of peace, calmness, joy, and fulfill-ment not a time of mulling over emotional re-actions.

The Emotional level of Mind is the sixth level of Mind. It is the level of Subconscious Mind closest to our physical existence and the Conscious Mind. So do not remain only in the emotional or sixth level of conscious-ness. Rather go beyond this to the deeper levels of mind, the fifth, fourth, and third levels. Then go beyond these to Superconscious Mind.

While a university student Patrick had this memorable meditation, truly an insightful look into the inner creative process of consciousness.

My attention was focused on becoming aware of the inner silence. As I was focusing my attention inward I focused on the space between the thoughts that passed through my mind. Suddenly it was as though I slipped through its motion into a

*tremendous energy. I felt as though I was sitting under a
roaring waterfall. The water or energy moved through every
cell of my body. It was thunderous.*

*I recall the thought drifting by of how contrary it seemed to
meditate on silence and enter into this thunderous experience.
The room was so loud in my mind though the thought was gone
like a leaf going over Niagara Falls.*

It felt right. It felt good.

I went with it.

*What I realized upon coming back is that the silence is
more than a void, it is pure potential. It is a vast infinite energy
that can become anything. It is like a canvas for an artist.*

This is a very inspiring meditation that inspires not only the meditator but the one who reads of this experience. In the classes at the School of Metaphysics the student is taught to still the mind. When this occurs there are no thoughts being produced in the conscious mind. Patrick had reached a point where he was able to slow his conscious mind thoughts enough to discern when one thought finished and another thought began. Then he focused on the interim or period between when one thought stopped and another thought started. At that time he experienced tremendous energy and realized why this is so. One who controls the mind controls all energy for thought is cause and the physical existence is the world of effects.

When the mind is stilled and the Self is free to enter the silence then the power, knowledge, and continual forward, motion of creation is experienced. It is humanity's duty to learn to harness this continual, forward, motion for the betterment of all and in order that soul growth can be enhanced.

The vast energy of creation is always available to be used. It remains for the thinker to prepare the mind to use it. The history of civilization is the story of learning to harness and use greater and higher types of energy. Starting with manpower, horsepower, waterpower, windpower, steampower, internal combustion engine power, electricity, and nuclear energy and solar power, and many more. Some day mankind will tap the energy of the sun, and then the galaxy and then the entire Universe. By the time the final stage is reached mankind will have evolved to a much higher form and will probably not even need or desire a physical body anymore.

Until that time arrives, it is important to understand and use the emotions productively. In reality it is the productive use of the Mind that will ultimately bring about the full use of energies. Learning to wield emotional energies to manifest your desires and creations teaches you about the vast creative energies available to you.

When the emotions are not being used productively these same emotions begin to impinge upon your meditation. You may find your Self experiencing anger during your meditation. This is almost always due to an undisciplined mind. When you are not creating in your daily life, your frustrated conscious mind begins to point this out to you as you sit there trying to meditate. Your failures and frustrations begin to come to the forefront of your mind. You start getting emotional about a time in the past that you did not get what you wanted. You wanted the raise or promotion on your job but didn't get it. You wanted the affection of a good looking acquaintance but did not get it and so on. You become emotionally angry at the person, persons, or reasons in your life that you perceive or blame as keeping you from having or getting what you want.

At these times still your mind and focus on mentally listening for the answer to your prayer or petition given at the beginning of meditation. It is also important that having identified your frustration, doubt, anger, fear, or worry that you take steps to rectify the situation by creating what you need in your daily life. Notice I said need, and not desire or want because your needs are few but your desires are limitless. You can spend a whole lifetime trying to fulfill one desire after another accumulating more and more physical objects. You may be very emotionally attached to these objects but in the end these physical objects will not give you enlightenment or Self understanding. The Emotional level of Mind is so close to the physical existence and Conscious Mind that everyone experiences the emotions while in their waking life. Everyone has had some experience with emotions. You have experienced not only your own emotions but the emotions of others. The emotions can be either pleasant or unpleasant depending upon your attitude or frame of mind and the particular emotion experienced.

The Emotional level of Mind must be respected by being utilized regularly and consistently in order for your ideas to manifest consistently and regularly as creations in your life. When the emotions are not being used, are avoided, suppressed, or ignored they then distract you from your meditation. When you meditate your attention moves inward from the conscious mind to the subconscious mind and you begin to experience emotions. You first encounter your unused, misused, or avoided emotions. This is why some people, when they first start meditation or when they begin to go deeper within during meditation encounter emotional states of being.

When emotions arise in meditation they are to be released by returning the attention to the point of devotion which is on listening for the answer to your prayer, petition, or question given in meditation. Later, when the meditation is completed you may give your attention to the emotions and reflect on them.

In order to successfully meditate one must learn the meaning of being still. As long as you are busy with the thought of the mind, as long as your thoughts are moving rapidly you will re-act emotionally. Recognize that when emotions arise during meditation it is the conscious mind and the conscious ego's effort to maintain control. Your habits and small thinking are controlling you.

One needs to transcend Self imposed limitations in order to understand the emotions and thoughts of Self. You do not come to understand the emotions or what is causing the emotional re-action by dwelling in the emotions. Rather when emotions appear in meditation give them no attention and allow them to pass through. Over time you will learn to transcend the emotions and the Emotional level of Mind and go deep into Subconscious Mind. Then, over time, you will go even deeper than this. You will transcend both your conscious and subconscious minds and evolve into Superconscious Mind.

If emotions persist and continue to distract you during meditation then remember the following three keys. Continually practice and apply them in your daily life.

1. *constantly create*
2. *use every situation to the fullest*
3. *always give*

Also remember that the more you speak your thoughts as they arise the more control you will have over your thoughts and emotions. The emotions are a way to complete the thoughts they are not the cause of your thoughts.

Meditation is not only a process of growth, it is also a process of unfolding and opening up. A flower can never be a flower until the bud opens up. Neither can a physically engrossed person become a spiritually enlightened being until an opening up and flowering of the Self occurs.

A closed-off or protective person is not very successful at meditation.

How does one begin the process of opening the Self? The answer is by learning to be at peace with Self and others and by pursuing a course of Self knowledge and Self understanding. Traci's experience describes this well.

> *This morning, Saturday of SOMA Conference, I had an excellent experience in meditation. I was able to still my mind enough to know where I could direct my attention to fully listen.*
>
> *It was as if I was having a conversation. My attention drifted several times, yet it went to topics I desired insight on. I received images and interpreted them in the Universal Language of Mind and was able to reason out guidance on what I can do for these areas in my life.*
>
> *I was at ease and I finally had a true desire to listen to my inner Self and hold my attention at the spiritual eye.*
> *The meditation lasted three times longer than my normal meditations, and I experienced a group consciousness of unity.*

Traci has been meditating for a few months and has shown tremendous progress during that time. Although she has not learned to still her mind at all times in meditation she has learned to bring her attention back to listening for the answer to her question when it does wander. She has developed the mental will power necessary to do this. The Universal Language of Mind is the language the inner subconscious mind utilizes to communicate with the conscious mind.

Because she had a true desire to listen to her inner Self she was able to meditate three times longer than her normal meditations. Desire is one of the necessary requirements for successful meditation. There must be a burning, overwhelming desire to know the inner Self and to discipline the Self and the conscious mind to do so.

The spiritual eye is the eye of perception also known as the third eye or the pituitary gland. It is located between and slightly above the two physical eyes. When meditating the gaze needs to be directed upward to the point between the eyebrows to the third eye, the eye of perception the pituitary. This aids in removing the attention from the physical eyes and other physical senses and focuses the attention instead on perception and perceiving with the mind which leads to an expansion of consciousness and an awareness of the inner light.

Traci's focus on the light of attention in the eye of perception enabled her to expand her consciousness beyond her physical body to the whole group of meditators. At this point her consciousness came together with the other meditators. At that time there ceased to be any walls between her and the others so it was as if they were all ONE and she experienced a unity of consciousness.

When we identify with the physical body then the mind focuses on the physical body. Since all physical bodies are separated by space we think of ourselves as alone. Even when we physically touch another still it is only a partial touching. However, when touching another with the mind the touching can be complete and total. Then it is like you and the other, or you and creation, or you and the Creator, are one. You realize you are not alone and you will never be alone again because you have expanded your mind to encompass all.

There needs to be the regular practice of meditation in order to receive into the Self the kind of awareness Traci is experiencing. This is a much greater and deeper awareness of the Real Self. Then the expression of emotions can be used to fulfill and complete desires rather than simply a way of gaining attention or blowing off pressure.

There is nothing to fear in meditation because the inner Self is good and beautiful. When fear controls you, your emotions run amok and this interferes with the meditation. Embrace change instead of fearing change for meditation will initiate the process of the transformation for the Self from a physical person to a spiritual person. Approach newness with an attitude of openness rather than the closed mindedness of combat.

The more completely one utilizes the emotions the more one will be able to receive, and therefore, increase the intuitive abilities and deepen one's meditation. Using the emotions does not mean regurgitating the same unpleasant emotions over and over. Using the emotions is a way of completing or fulfilling the desires and the thoughts rather than simply getting rid of something that has built up within the Self. You need to be intentional in the expression of Self verbally, emotionally, and thoughtfully. The emotions are a vehicle for developing oneness and unity with your neighbors. The emotions are not meant to be a tool to blow someone away or to overpower them.

There is a difference between emotional honesty and emotional manipulation. Emotional honesty improves and enhances your oneness with others while emotional manipulation makes people want to get away from you. In order to have charisma one must be willing to give emotionally. Charisma is the art of having a clear thought in Mind and moving this thought through Subconscious Mind, through the emotions and all the way out into the physical existence. When this process is used efficiently, others will catch your expansive thought and be thrilled.

Blaming others is due to being stubborn emotionally. Remember, you create your life. You have free will. It is through your choices that you created your life as it is today. Bad luck is due to blame, casting blame on others or on your environment. When you accept that you are the cause of your life then and only then do you have the power to change your life to be the way you desire it to be. Mental and emotional causes are not a point of blame, rather this is a point of recognition or awareness of the need to change on the part of the individual. Each person causes their own situations, circumstances, and re-actions.

During suppression of the emotions the person is out of control and not in control because such a person is not even aware of what is being brought to the awareness. In other words, you are so caught up in your own problems and re-actions that you do not even see or perceive what is actually going on around you. Instead you filter everything through the falsity of your anger, blame, fear, and self-pity.

The emotions are not a way to re-act to the world but instead are a way to act or take action in the world. The emotions are not a cause they are an effect. Transcend the emotions do not avoid them. Anger is caused by refusing to understand the cause of one's own way of thinking. Meditation gives you the ability to know your thoughts. You will gain control of the emotions when you gain better understanding of your own thinking.

Depression is the result of emotional denial. When one sets an ideal for the Self, there is a positive image to work toward. Then there is no place for worry about the future for one will be creating his or her future.

Recognize that physical proximity is not a requirement for Love. It is not a requirement for communication. It is not a requirement for bonds whether familial or divine. What is a requirement for this is a desire, a mutual understanding, commitment, and loyalty, and above all, honesty.

Instead of trying to be everything to everyone, identify what you uniquely have to offer or give. Be the director more than the actor of your life.

It is not physical time that is important in the scope of one's soul progression and evolution; it is the choices that are made and how rich the life is from those choices. Therefore, set the attention, value, and activities in life on the richness of the experiences and understanding rather than their duration.

Realize condemnation adds to one's grief.

Sympathy is taking on the difficulties of others.

Empathy is the direct perception of understanding someone else's experience.

Make empathy an understanding within the Self.

Accept the Self as is, and move forward.

An adult person experiences mental and emotional pain due to selfishness. Give more and the pain begins to subside.

Not being able to achieve one's desires often comes from avoiding, ignoring, and being afraid of the emotions. A person needs to learn to state openly and honestly what he or she is thinking and experiencing. In this way you come out from inside of yourself and break the vicious cycle of habitual, repetitive thoughts.

Emotions are a pushing force, a power that causes our creations to manifest into the physical existence which is our daily lives. When an emotion is exhibited look for what has been created. If nothing was created the expression of that emotion was a waste. The only thing that occurred was letting off of pressure that had been bottled up in the emotions due to the person having unproductive, habitual, and limiting thoughts. When one is directing the conscious mind with will and imagination and concentration, and discipline then the emotions can be used productively for charisma and other kinds of creations. The individual is not meant to be a pressure cooker that builds up steam. The energy of the Real Self is meant to flow fluidly and easily from the mental

Self to the emotional Self to the physical Self.

The proper use of emotion is consciously creating a thought form and emoting it when it reaches the sixth level of consciousness. Emote the thought form from the sixth level of Mind, the Emotional level to the seventh level of Mind the Conscious or physical level.

Emotions are not the cause rather the emotions are the effect of the thoughts one has created and are a means of transport for the thoughts of Self rather than being an end in themselves. The emotions are the means by which one manifests the cause which is thought. Emotions are the vehicle by which one can manifest one's own thinking from the inner levels of Mind. Not being able to achieve or manifest one's desires is often from avoiding, ignoring, and being afraid of the emotions. You need to state openly and honestly what you are thinking.

Emotional expression is a natural part of the Self and can be productive. Practice laughing and smiling. Emotional release is a hard and difficult way to change because it relies on memory instead of imagination. When you try to suppress the emotions they get the better of you. Mental passivity produces emotional aggression.

By being in action the mind learns the value of stillness. Consider the following.

My first experience with fasting and silence and meditation for an extended period of time came during a Commitment Weekend at the College of Metaphysics. Dr. Dan (Condron) gave us instruction and a workbook, and told us if we followed the instructions step by step that we would hear the silence and go deeper in meditation than we had before.

Saturday around midnight I was doing my last meditation, I had been building expectation and anticipation throughout the day. A little earlier I had been outside in the dark gazing awestruck at the beauty and brightness of the stars. I went into my tent and began my meditation, with the expectation that this would be my deepest experience thus far. As I stilled my mind, I suddenly became aware of total silence. I didn't hear insects or frogs or cows or any other noise. I was experiencing total silence!

As I basked in the silence in profound peace and serenity, I

again marveled at the beauty of the stars in the moonless night
sky. The stars were so brilliant against the black sky. I could
even see the Milky Way.

Then I suddenly remembered I was not outside anymore
looking at the sky, I was inside my tent, and from that vantage
point I should not be able to see stars. With that thought I
came back to my tent and back to my physical body, but for
these moments I experienced total peace and freedom and
peace and unity with creation.

Karen's experience was the result of a series of mental actions. Daily meditation times served to prepare the way for this experience. Consistently directing the mind in meditation creates the calmness that allows realization in the outer consciousness.

Immediately preceding this meditation she directed her mind in several physical experiences. Cleansing the body by taking in only water and no solid foods. Making the time and space in the life to join with others who also desire communion with their Creator. Responding to instructions from one more experienced. Each decision directed mental, and therefore emotional, energies toward the fulfillment of her ideal.

In the fruition of her ideal she found the stillness she had dreamed of, the silence that can only be heard within. Mental clarity. Emotional calmness. Physical relaxation. Stillness swept through her being, freeing her consciousness from being entrapped in the physical body.

The subconscious mind is not limited like the conscious mind is. The conscious mind is restricted to the physical body and the five senses. The five senses cannot see through a tent to see the stars but the subconscious mind can perceive as far as the thinker can image, imagine and conceive.

In meditation you can literally learn to "see", perceive, through walls because physical walls are of their very nature physical while the subconscious mind is beyond the physical and utilizes direct perception. Your understanding and control of your emotions determines in large part your capacity to experience the inner levels of consciousness and once there to remain there for as long as desired to explore, to learn, to be.

1

I sometimes have emotional experiences in meditation that distract me. How do I move beyond this?

By recognizing this is just your conscious ego attempting to control you. When distracting thoughts or emotions arise from thoughts say to your conscious mind, "No, I do not desire to think these negative and limiting thoughts." "Now I choose to place my undivided attention on listening to the answer to my prayer." "This is a time of great peace for me."

Gradually or quickly your conscious mind will become trained to do as you, the thinker, direct it to do.

2

When I move my attention into the sixth level of Mind sometimes I resist going all the way in. How can I move past this?

Throughout the day learn to share your thoughts, feelings, ideas, and emotions with others in a joyful, peaceful manner. Recognize you are not a physical body, therefore, you do not need your physical body in meditation. You will expand beyond your physical body in meditation to your room, your city, your country, your planet and finally to the entire universe.

3

What is occurring when I meditate and tears begin to flow from my eyes non-stop and the experience is pleasant and calming?

You meditated and brought your attention to the physical, realizing you had been crying. What is the cause of this? Your soul is crying with joy that you finally came home. Your inner Self is overjoyed that you are listening to the Real Inner You.

4

What should a good meditation feel like? Look like? Be like?

The most beautiful, the most delicious fruit nectar you have ever tasted. The most joyous experience you have ever had. The greatest, deepest experience of love you have ever had. In other words everything and all you have experienced good in the world meditation provides only deeper and better. Meditation should be the most peaceful experience, the most pleasant adventure, the most joyful and blissful time you have ever been in or been through. In really deep, good, meditation you want it to last forever.

5

Sometimes I feel a very deep love I wish to understand and know what this feeling is related to and how to have it more often.

This is the love of your Soul, your inner Self for the you existing and entrapped in the physical body and physical environment. Meditate regularly and often and deeply and you will gain this love more often and even more deeply. It is related to your whole Self. It is related to your superconscious mind. It is related to all of Creation.

6

How can one get past destructive emotions?

Meditate every day. Imagine a different way of being for the Self and choose different, more positive and productive people to associate with and to form friendships with. Associate with souls who have ideals that are in alignment with the more productive, positive, spiritual ideals that you want to develop within yourself.

7

How do I keep myself from falling into emotional negativity such as anger, depression, sadness, and self-pity?

Think about the good and positive things you want and desire to occur now and in the future. Do not allow your mind to dwell on hurts of the past. You cannot change the past. When you can identify an anger or hurt coming on in your mind and can change the thought to the joy of what you want to create then you will have control of your mind and therefore, your emotions.

8

What is the difference between suppression of emotions and emotional control?

Emotional control is the awareness of how energy moves and how the thoughts and feelings are in relationship to how to direct the emotion or feeling that is being felt. The suppression of emotion is, in effect, denying that the thoughts or feelings even exist. Therefore, the energy behind the thoughts continues to build up until a person experiences what one has experienced in the past such as emotional outbursts.

9

When one is out of control emotionally what is the best thing to do?

Still the mind.

10

For long term understanding, use, and control of the emotions what do I do?

Think very deeply about the nature of your soul. Remove your attention from pain and direct it toward Self as soul. Learn to identify and fulfill the needs of the Soul. This is what will cause there to be forward motion in the Self and in the life.

Chapter Seven

Group Consciousness
in Subconscious and Superconscious Minds

Have you ever felt alone? Have you ever felt like you were separate and apart from everything else? Loneliness is an unpleasant feeling. It is an emptiness. When you are lonely it feels like your life has no purpose and meaning.

Loneliness is a product of a materialistic and physical concept of the world. If you accept the idea that all there is to life is what you experience with the five senses, then a tree is separate from you because it is separate from your physical body which you think is you. A cow is separate from you. Green grass is separate from you. The sky is separate from you. The planet Earth is separate from you and all the people you meet; your friends, relatives and co-workers are separate from you. Such a world view is a lonely existence.

In meditation you experience the Universal Truth and the Truth is this: you are an intimate part of God, the Creator's Creation. You are an important part of the Eternal's Creation.

As you dive deeper and deeper into meditation your consciousness will expand to more and more of creation until your consciousness and awareness has expanded to all of creation. Then you will know the Creator. You will do much more than see God face to face as Moses did while looking at the burning bush. You will embrace the Creator and fully experience boundless love. For the Eternal's love fills all of creation. You will commune and communicate with the Creator. Let love be pure and flow without restriction. Care and love all creation because it is you.

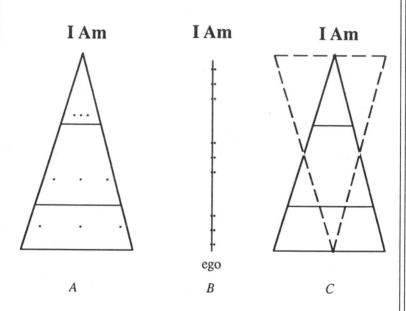

Diagram 9.

I Am   I Am   I Am

A   B   C

ego

A   = *Average physically entrapped person who does not know anything of the inner levels of Mind or the interconnectedness between all people and all creation.*

B   = *Individual who has achieved stillness of the Mind and recognizes the unity of Self and all Creation.*

C   = *Individual who knows and understands I AM and has expanded his or her consciousness to serve all, give to, and teach all humanity. A World Teacher and a World Server. Dotted lines indicate one who has achieved Cosmic Consciousness.*

All I AMs have group consciousness in Superconscious Mind and to a lesser extent in Subconscious Mind. In Mind we are all connected and interconnected. The deeper into Mind you go the more this interconnectedness is apparent. Then the phrase or statement, "we are all one" comes to have more meaning and you perceive the certitude of it. We are all one does not mean we have lost our identity and individuality as if some giant amoeba has absorbed us. Rather it means that we not only recognize our interconnectedness but that we are aware of the connection and interconnectedness and live our lives with this clear understanding and perception.

Diagram 9 shows how consciousness manifests from the Superconscious Mind through the Subconscious Mind and into the physical existence or Conscious Mind.

Bliss begins with *B* and builds and increases through *C*. As you move forward from *B* to *C* the *Thrill of Creation* is achieved. You are gaining compatibility with your Creator and becoming a Creator yourself.

By giving to all others through service one breaks down the walls of separateness and then abides in the natural state of connectedness with all people and all creation. All minds in Union are known as Bliss.

Isolation is not a natural part of Creation. Interconnectedness is natural and normal. It is the natural action of Creation. You may not see it when you are physically engrossed but it works and functions throughout Creation. One person's enlightenment affects every other person in Creation. This interconnectedness occurs and functions through the Universal Laws of Creation such as the Law of Cause and Effect, the Law of Infinity, and the Complete Law. As your mind expands to receive more and more of Creation then more and more awareness of Consciousness becomes available to you.

Most people are so caught up in their own problems, worries, guilts, fears, and desires that they leave little room for expanding their consciousness beyond themselves and their little world. The more you place your Self in positions in which you can associate with other people and give to more and more people on a larger scale the more and greater opportunities to discover your connectedness with others. You will also discover your connectedness with the Universal, Permanent, Eternal, quality of Self.

Subconscious Mind and Universal Mind

Have you ever visited the library? If you have then you know from experience that the library provides you with information gleaned from thousands of sources that you would not otherwise have access to.

You may access various points in history through the use of the library. Suppose you want to find out about Abraham Lincoln. You may look for him under the letter *L* for Lincoln or *P* for presidents of the United States of America or *C* for Civil War as he led our country through the Civil War.

You may also learn a lot about geography at the library. You can check out books that show all the continents and oceans of planet Earth as well as the various countries. You can also find the locations of countries that existed hundreds or thousands of years ago that no longer exist. You can compare how the face of the world map changes even now, as governments dissolve and are reestablished, agreements made, lands sold, exchanged or stolen.

There is a Universal Truth that may be stated thusly, AS ABOVE, SO BELOW. This in essence means, that for everything created in the physical, material, gross world of substance there is a mental, or spiritual or inner mind counterpart that is actually the true or real thing of creation. This truth also means that all creation begins with a thought and that thoughts are things and they are real and have reality and substance.

Just as we have physical libraries so there is a great Universal Library called the Akashic Library or more appropriately, the Akashic Records.

The Akashic Records stored or housed in Subconscious or Universal Mind are a permanent record of everything that has ever been said, thought, and done. One who is able to access this Universal Library of Mind has before him or her an accurate history and universal knowledge.

It was not part of Jane's consciousness to devote daily time to meditation, and the following experience demonstrates the extremes that can result. Here she recalls a meditative experience induced externally and influenced by the company of others; reflecting the power of group consciousness. As you will see, she was ill-prepared for what was revealed to her.

I was watching a video of group meditation, then chanting and finally meditating. I saw in meditation a scroll, a foot high, rolled with beautiful words on it.

It was such a perfect meditation. Unfortunately, I was getting extremely sick and left after a few minutes. I was totally purged each hour for twelve hours.

I'm awaiting this type of experience - the Scrolling message again. Other graphic experiences have been a beautiful eye looking at me. It was very expressive and loving. Know I received a deep message from it as the peace and contentment was wonderful.

Fortunately, Jane's times of meditation, although inconsistent, had brought her enough knowledge and wisdom to see the potential and the beauty in the glimpse she received. A lesser person would have become entrapped in the reactions of the body and missed the insights she achieved.

The scroll in Jane's meditation symbolizes the Akashic Records also called the Hall of Learning, the Hall of Knowledge, and the Universal Library. This place exists in Subconscious Mind where records of everything that has been said, thought, and done are impressed. Jane's scroll symbolizes the Hall of Records, located at the mid-point of Subconscious or Universal Mind. The fact that the scroll started to unroll shows that she was accessing, or reading, these Akashic records.

One who meditates regularly, over time, learns to release the conscious mind and to go deeper and deeper within to subconscious mind. There he begins to be able to perceive this Universal Knowledge of Mind and is capable of receiving the Wisdom of the Ages. Instead of being limited in their information and experience to only what is stored in their brain he or she now has an expanded consciousness that is capable of receiving the accumulated knowledge of millions of people over thousands and tens of thousands of years.

Where is this Akashic Records you may ask? The Akashic Records are located between the fourth and fifth levels of Mind the midpoint of the Subconscious Mind. It is the point where mental ideas that are in the process of manifestation begin to take on physical form.

The Akashic Records and Universal Mind have also been referred to at various times and places as the Hall of Records, Hall of Knowledge, and by the phrase, "In my father's house are many mansions."

Different people, in different times, in different ways, to different degrees are and have been able to access and go to the Akashic Records located in Subconscious Mind.

What began as a beautiful, revelatory meditation experience for Jane ended in the purging effects of the limitations remaining in her outer, physical conscious mind. Her access to Universal Mind was not the result of her own preparation, changes in her own consciousness. Rather, all the chanting done before the meditation propelled her further into meditation than she had earned or was prepared for. What she was able to glimpse for a moment was a sign of what is to come and the abilities that she is capable of attaining by maintaining her commitment to her learning and growth.

Group Consciousness and Meditation

Each person needs to cause there to be heaven on earth. To accomplish this you must create or make your conscious mind be productive as is your subconscious mind. The Subconscious Mind knows only forward motion, learning, and growth. Your subconscious mind desires growth filled understandings to be built by your conscious mind so they can be stored as permanent memory in subconscious mind.

In Subconscious Mind all minds are connected. The telephone, its use and function, serve as an analogy to the interconnectedness experienced in Subconscious Mind. By using the telephone you have quick access to other people hundreds or thousands of miles away. Through the use of Subconscious or Universal Mind one's own subconscious mind can communicate with another person even though they are physically separated by great distances. What is required to send a message is a clear and specific mental image *plus* will power. What is required to receive the image is a still and quiet mind and receptivity. This is a kind of group consciousness, a universal interconnectedness with the opportunity and possibility of clear and open communication without the limitation of distance or space.

In Superconscious Mind, group consciousness is carried or advanced one step farther. In Superconscious Mind it is as if there is little or no

Communication, Contact, and Interconnectedness within the three Divisions of Mind by individual Souls or Beings

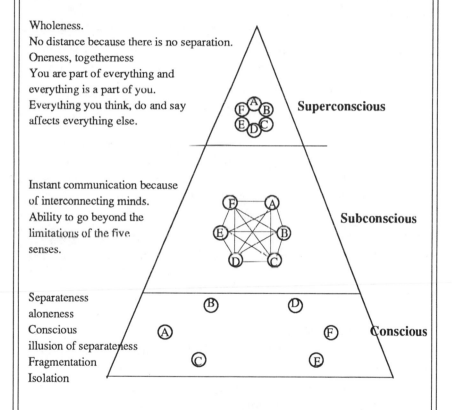

Wholeness.
No distance because there is no separation.
Oneness, togetherness
You are part of everything and
everything is a part of you.
Everything you think, do and say
affects everything else.

Superconscious

Instant communication because
of interconnecting minds.
Ability to go beyond the
limitations of the five
senses.

Subconscious

Separateness
aloneness
Conscious
illusion of separateness
Fragmentation
Isolation

Conscious

Diagram 10.

distance between individuals. Both distance and time as measured physically have little relevance. For time is measured mentally and there is no separation by distance. When the distance is removed we have Oneness. Therefore, in Superconscious Mind you experience Oneness. Oneness is group consciousness carried or evolved to its fulfillment.

When group consciousness is achieved there is no war, discord, or disharmony. When group consciousness exists there is a common Ideal and a common Purpose. Therefore, all are working together, and in harmony for the common good.

In meditation as you go deeper and deeper into Mind you will experience first an interconnectedness with all creation. As you gain depth in these meditations, this interconnectedness will blend into a Oneness, an experience of non-separation with all of creation including everyone and everything in creation. Then you will experience oneness with the Eternal Creator.

Since you would never harm yourself, you would not harm anyone else as all and everything is a part of the Eternal's Creation. You desire to be a co-creator, a helpmate to the Eternal. Your whole countenance is full of productive creation and you desire for all to evolve rapidly.

Your thoughts transcend thinking only of yourself and your selfish desires. Instead your consciousness expands to all of creation and helping all of mankind to evolve quickly to know the Supreme, the Eternal. No longer are you alone. No longer are you separate and disconnected from humanity and life. No longer do you feel cut off from others or cut off from life. No longer do you feel there is a wall between you and others. Since you are one with and communicate with all of creation you are able to create much more capably and expansively. In fact, you are a creator. The only thing that impedes your ability to cause creation to quicken, which is the highest form of creativity, is other people's free will and refusal to exercise the imagination.

Jesus (Joshua, Jeshua) of Nazareth who became the Christ (messiah) savior-enlightened, and Siddhartha Guatama, the Buddha who accomplished the enlightenment, also gave to the world their wisdom and understanding of how to cause rapid spiritual transformation and soul growth. However, millions of people have ignored or avoided these truths for thousands of years. Instead, they opt for entrapment in limited physical existence.

As you meditate this will change for you. Your consciousness will expand to fill all mind and you will know that every person is intimately connected with you. They are your spiritual brothers and sisters and it is your duty to help them find their way and earn their way to their spiritual home and spiritual family of Intuitive Man.

Meditation builds oneness and a knowing of oneness.

Physical thinking deludes one into thinking he or she is separate and therefore alone.

The expansive consciousness that creates the joy of oneness produces fulfillment in the life as well as purpose and meaning to the life.

Physical thinking leads to being possessed by the possessions you seek to accumulate. Physical thinking leads to a starving of the inner Self and a gnawing feeling that there is always something missing in life.

In expansive and deep meditation the impetus of the awareness of group consciousness is created. Then one is free and able to create.

It is important and necessary for soul growth that you create group consciousness in the outer physical world with many other people. By so doing you are causing the physical environment and your life to move into alignment with the inner life of Subconscious and Superconscious Minds. In this way you bring about Heaven on Earth.

To develop, create, and have group consciousness:

1. Create a common goal

*2. Recognize what you have to offer to the group
and each individual in the group and give it.*

*3. Have clear and productive communication.
Ask questions and listen.*

*4. To create a higher group consciousness
a) Have a common ideal
b) Have mental communication*

The vibration or "sound" of Creation is around us at all times. We have but to still the mind to be able to perceive and experience it. When you experience the silence then you will know your connection with God and all of Creation. Once you have experienced this interconnectedness with everyone and everything you will never want to go back to being the old limited you. You will recognize this interconnectedness more and more as you learn and grow in consciousness so that all of humanity benefits. As you aid others in their soul growth you will find the greatest fulfillment and come to understand the interconnectedness of all of humanity and all of Creation. As you are drawn to others – or draw others to you – of like mind who desire awareness of higher consciousness, you will find that you exist with your real, spiritual family. Then you will know your true soul mate.

To develop love and compassion, learn to be one with others. In order for there to be love there needs to be growth, change, and the expansion of consciousness. It is good to be needed. This can provide a sense of worth and value. Always remember to teach others to learn what you know so there is no dependency built. Help others to reach the next higher level in the soul understanding and awareness.

Thirty-three year old Angela, an accountant, had recently moved to Oklahoma City to take on a new position and be closer to her family. This was soon after the bombing of the Murrah Federal Building, the city was hurting and she knew it. She also knew helping heal that wound was a large part of why she had come.

> *I was on the large floral couch in the living area around midnight. I had chanted the "AUM".*
>
> *My petition had been "Dear God, aid me with direction as how to teach and heal within the city of OKC."*
>
> *Shortly after this I was engulfed within the most beautiful light. I had experienced this before, yet this time I was drawn to go beyond the Light and I perceived Intelligence;– this was the thought form, the essence of the vibration.*
>
> *The answer to my question I believe was to go forth and aid others with my own intelligent direction as well as relying on that of God.*

In her question for meditation, Angela had requested knowledge of how to aid others, specifically the people of the city of Oklahoma City, Oklahoma. Because she was thinking of others rather than just herself and seeking to help others to progress and learn and grow her consciousness was able to expand beyond her conscious mind and physical body.

She was engulfed in a light greater than her own conscious mind light. Because she expanded her desire and willingness to give she was able to expand her ability to receive to a higher level than she had ever before experienced. She was able to go beyond this expanded light which signifies the ability and willingness to go beyond previous limitations to achieve much more in life in aiding others to peace, prosperity, and abundance and also in gaining greater enlightenment for the Self.

The Conscious Ego

The word EGO means I AM. The I AM or identity that is you, your core essence, in using mind moves into first the Superconscious Mind, then Subconscious Mind, then the Conscious Mind. The attention of I AM moved through the levels and divisions of Mind until finally you became entrapped in the physical body and conscious mind. At this point the physically entrapped I AM is known as the conscious ego.

Therefore, every person has a conscious ego that is a reflection of I AM. The conscious ego has accepted the limitations of the conscious mind and physical body. However, there is a way out of these limitations of physical existence for the conscious ego is the motivator. On a physical level the conscious ego motivates you to achieve physical goals and accumulate or possess physical objects.

The average person allows their conscious ego to motivate them to achieve physical goals or to gather physical things about themselves. This does provide a certain amount of physical security but it does not expand one's consciousness beyond the physical existence. This leaves the average person with the feeling that something is missing from their life. They experience a dissatisfaction, an uneasiness, and a feeling of unfulfillment in the life. Then this kind of person tries to accumulate more physical possessions or fame and finds they are still unfulfilled.

The more evolved person recognizes that all physical, sensory objects and possessions are temporary and therefore, strives to use them to the fullest and shares them with others. The meditator strives and achieves the greater and true satisfaction of knowing inner, Real Self.

As the meditator learns to dive deeper into mind he finds the satisfaction and fulfillment with life increasing.

One must surrender the conscious mind ego so the whole Self and the whole Mind can evolve. To evolve you must give freely to all and thereby become a part of all and have a consciousness that encompasses all. This is not possible as long as you have a wall of protection around yourself.

There comes a time in each person's evolution when they must surrender their conscious ego. Each person must surrender. As long as you are fighting or defending yourself, offensive or defensive, you cannot receive for you have erected mental barriers of seeming protection around you. You are incapable of receiving the blessings of the I AM. You are not capable of receiving the blessings of the High Self or Superconscious Mind Self.

To receive the love of the Creator that uplifts one's consciousness one must learn to receive. One must learn to let the walls of protection down and become completely open. This may at first seem like you are vulnerable. The very idea of vulnerability indicates you see your environment as your enemy. In mind, however, the Creator's protective love is more pronounced. The deeper you go into mind the closer you are to the Eternal, the all-encompassing love of the Creator.

An English as a Second Language Instructor, Mari recalls a meditation experience that happened a decade ago as if it happened yesterday. And indeed in a way it did, because the impact of that long ago meditation enabled her to establish a communion with her Creator that has grown ever since.

> *My greatest meditation experience since entering into the School of Metaphysics was about eight years ago when I saw and heard the voice I've come to recognize as **God's voice**.*
>
> *I was very centered and calm. I realized I'd finally learned how to meditate after struggling with it for quite some time. I felt a great transcendence and love and peace. I don't remember the thoughts I heard, but it was clear and real and an answer to me. It was the time I felt I'd really broken through all my barriers. It was truly heavenly.*

God is always near us and with us. A still and quiet mind is necessary to hear God. The deeper you go into Mind the more you experience love and peace. Peace is a factor of unity, togetherness, and harmony. All these are a part of the basic structure of Superconscious Mind. The Mind triangle diagram has shown how the top of the triangle is narrower or closer together than the bottom symbolizing the closeness or togetherness, or unity of the Superconscious Mind.

The experience of Superconscious Mind is heavenly. In fact, Superconscious Mind is Heaven. This is why you can learn to experience heaven on earth. All the great enlightened beings of earth have experienced heaven while still in a physical incarnation. In meditation their mind would transcend, expand, and go beyond physical limitations and experience Heaven or Superconscious Mind.

When you experience Superconscious Mind you truly have broken through all barriers and it is truly heavenly. The next step is to learn to experience Superconscious Mind regularly and consistently.

Meditation is a receptive action. In the act of meditation you, the meditator, release your limitations and walls of physical protectiveness and travel deep within to be one with the Creator's love.

In meditation, the mind expands to fill all creation. There is no need for exclusiveness or closing off to the love of creation. In deep meditation you receive the Christ Consciousness that is available to everyone on the planet that so few are willing receive.

As conscious mind stillness harmonizes with Subconscious Mind and then aligns with Superconscious Mind the Christ Consciousness becomes yours and you know your connectedness with all Creation. You understand your purpose. You understand your assignment for this lifetime and your love for God and all Creation expands into the boundless joy and bliss of full connectedness of existence in the Creator's all-encompassing love.

You can remain locked up and limited in the conscious ego's physical motivation and walls of protection or you can free yourself and go beyond time and space to the limitless abundance and expansive Christ Consciousness of Union. Then all of creation and everything in it is yours for you are a guardian of Creation.

You can have anything you desire. People usually get what they want. The problem arises because their consciousness is limited and they therefore, desire limited things that only end up restricting and limiting them. They desire things that aren't good for them.

Cause your physical wants to elevate to inner, mental desires. Cause mental desires to expand to spiritual needs for soul growth and spiritual development.

The one who meditates consistently and correctly finds their consciousness lifted and their perception heightened so they gain greater understanding of the meaning life and their part in it. Then strive closer and closer and in a deeper way to become a helpmate in God's Creation.

The Unproductive Ego

The conscious ego is intended to be the motivator for the conscious mind. The conscious ego is the physical or seventh level of mind manifestation or embodiment of I AM = EGO.

The conscious ego is productive when it is pursuing harmony and alignment with I AM. The conscious ego is productive when there is honesty with Self and others for honesty is a prerequisite for understanding truth, especially and including Universal Truth. The individual's thoughts and words must match otherwise there exists an unhealthy conscious ego.

An unhealthy or unproductive conscious ego ignores the inner Self and has placed its security in conscious mind manipulations of others in an attempt to take, grab, and steal as many things, possessions, people, money, and objects that it can.

The unproductive conscious ego has forgotten who he is. Instead of existing as a spiritual being he acts as a cunning animal: a wolf masquerading in sheep's clothing. Since the person with the unproductive ego thinks only in physical ways such a person only has physical goals and no spiritual Ideals. Such a person has accepted that their physical, sensory, experience is all there is to existence and at death he or she ceases to exist. Therefore, such a one wants to grab and take as much physical security or things that he can, right now. He does this in any way he can, honestly or not.

The spiritualized individual, the one with an honest, productive, conscious ego, recognizes they are a soul inhabiting a physical body. The body is temporary while the Real Self is eternal. Therefore, the spiritualized being gives his time, attention, and value to the True Self, the Eternal Self.

Every action taken in the physical day to day life is used to add to one's storehouse of understandings and to build higher levels of awareness in the spiritualized Self. This is why two people can be doing the same activity for vastly different reasons. One person may teach for money while another teaches because he honestly and sincerely cares about other people's learning, growth and well-being. One person may dig ditches to make money to spend it on sensory gratification while another person uses the money for soul growth to aid a spiritualized organization and to help others.

By a man's actions and thoughts is his or her conscious ego known. The conscious ego is not always known by the words he or she uses, for people can memorize pretty words. A conscious ego, however, can not say these truths from the heart for they do not exist in such a person's heart. They exist in the physical brain and its memories. The brain dies at the end of each lifetime while the heart is the center of understanding which is eternal.

You the meditative being are blessed with having a way to come to know your true inner Self. You will learn to transcend the conscious ego to first know the subconscious ego then the superconscious ego and finally I AM-EGO. Then you will know I AM and will exist in permanent, full consciousness and awareness of your Creator and all of Creation. You will be cosmic and Universal in Nature. You will know all Universal Laws and Truths. You will know the Principles that create these Laws and Truths. Your Universal, Enlightened Love will pour down upon humanity like a golden shower of glistening, gold, raindrops and you will be a World Server, a World Teacher. You will receive and know the Christ Consciousness that is available to those who prepare themselves to receive it.

Cause your meditation to deepen each day as you grow in awareness. Be committed to your learning and growth. Cause your meditation to be the best part of each day; a fountain of water that refreshes you like nothing else. Let meditation be for you a stream of life giving water. While all sensory experiences are temporary and stimulate you only for a few moments recognize that the eternal creation gained in meditation gives you eternal joy, fulfillment, happiness, peace, satisfaction, love, and wisdom.

Meditating
with Attention on the Third Eye and the Heart

The body has three areas or "brains" that can be, and need to be, utilized in meditation. Those three areas are the head, heart, and spine. The head area's main points of focus in mediation are the pituitary also known as the brow chakra or third eye and the pineal gland having to do with the crown chakra.

The spinal column is the area of the body that connects the lower functions to the higher functions. The spinal column and the fluids within provide the vehicle or avenue for the energies of the Superconscious mind to be brought into and manifested in the physical existence.

The heart is the third center of intelligence in the body and is used and tied in closely with the process of building understandings in the Self. The heart chakra is first activated or quickened as the entrapped soul dedicates and commits the Self to soul growth in the current lifetime. Understanding is the key quality of the Heart. As the evolvement of the advanced soul progresses, the light of the heart center increases and the individual comes to know that the purpose of physical incarnation is to build understandings.

As one becomes more and more like a creator and every action becomes a creation in service to our Creator and as the life is filled with aiding others to climb the ladder of soul growth the enlightenment in the crown of the head touches the understanding in the heart and the two are from then on intimately and ultimately connected. The Self resides in the heart in full enlightenment and with full connectedness to the Creator. Such a one walks in full awareness of creation and Creator. Such a one exists in full harmonious loving creation with the Creator. Such a one has become a full helpmate in furthering the fulfillment of the Eternal's Creation so all may be raised to the level of God Consciousness.

To truly understand Transcendental Meditation you must first heal yourself. If there is any dichotomy left within you at this time it must be purged. You cannot think one thing and do or say another and expect to enter deep into meditation. You must be honest, truthful, kind, caring, and giving in order to enter deep into meditation and into the kingdom of the Supreme Creator. As you learn cooperation with Self and others then Self discipline will come easily.

The healing must be permanent. Any negative, limited, selfish, unproductive thought and attitude must be eliminated. One is most capable of receiving the healing which is permanent and good when the mind is still and the body is relaxed and still also.

Most people have a distance between the way they intellectually think and the way they live in the heart. There is a need to bridge the gap to relieve the yearning and pain. When the spark of divine wisdom is lit in a person's heart then he or she is aroused to direct the Self to learn the meaning of Life, from a teacher who can teach her of Mind and Self.

The benefits of meditating on the Heart are that this creates a type of blend of the lower consciousness with the higher consciousness. This has the effect of combining or harmonizing these levels of consciousness together. Later you will go beyond this. The benefits of connecting the crown chakra with the heart chakra are that this can produce an acceleration of awareness and therefore enlightenment. This is due to the fact that the understandings are being offered to a Higher level of awareness.

Meditation and the Conscious Ego

Surrendering the conscious ego must occur in order for the individual to expand his or her consciousness. The conscious ego is by its very nature limited for it functions in the conscious mind and through that, the physical existence.

The only reason for not surrendering the conscious ego is you think you are at war with your environment and everyone in it. Therefore, you think you have to protect yourself. Your conscious ego is the way you as I AM manifest in the physical existence.

An ego at war with the world whether accepting a defensive or offensive position is always protective. This runs contrary to the nature of the Universe. The nature of the Universe is interconnectedness and without barriers. We each have our own identity and unique individuality and we are all intimately interconnected. This is why whatever you do affects the entire universe.

To expand your consciousness in meditation you can have no walls of separation or protection between you and all the universe including spiritual, mental, emotional, and physical. When there are no walls and no barriers and you realize the full interconnectedness then there is receptivity.

A protected ego and surrendering the ego are mutually exclusive. The conscious ego must be surrendered so you may expand your consciousness into all of mind instead of only the seventh level, physical existence.

The conscious ego, your small self will be left behind as you expand your knowledge, wisdom, understanding and consciousness into the totality of I AM.

A protected ego and receptivity are mutually exclusive. Therefore, in meditation always be receptive. Be ready, prepared, and expectantly listening for the answer to your prayer, question, or petition. Ask for help in quickening the evolutionary process within yourself as well as solving your temporary physical problems.

Leave your small self, your conscious ego, behind in meditation and expand to the High Self which is the greater you. Learn who you really are in meditation. Discover your assignment for this lifetime and gain a glimpse of who you will become.

1

Are there greater benefits in group meditation or individual meditation sessions?

Each individual needs to learn to meditate every day in their own quiet place. This should be a room or part of a room set aside just for meditation. The student should learn to discipline the body and still the mind. There should be no movement during meditation.

Group meditation may be used occasionally as an adjunct to individual meditation for it stimulates the desire for greater and deeper meditation. Group meditation combines the thought forms of many people to create a very powerful thought form that the new meditator can make use of. Ultimately you must do the meditation. No one else can do it for you although others can help you tremendously.

2

What is occurring with my mediation experience when I feel inflated and large in the room? How can I use this?

Your consciousness is expanding. This is a good sign of progress. Your ideal is to expand to fill first your room, then your city or state then your country, then planet Earth, and then the entire Universe. When your consciousness fills to and expands to the entire Universe you have Cosmic Consciousness or Superconscious Meditation.

3

I desire to teach my understanding of group con-sciousness to all people. How do I teach it to someone who doesn't even understand the concept of being courteous to others?

Stop trying to boss other people around and instead be a friend to that person and to other people. Then you will begin to build group consciousness.

4

Will I lose my identity in group consciousness?

The purpose of group consciousness is not to lose anything.
      The purpose of group consciousness is to increase the strength and power of our minds by having a common ideal and purpose. This quickens spiritual evolution. This enhances the mental connections be-tween you and all others so people can work together to achieve enlightenment.

5

How can a strong, unified group consciousness be created in any situation? (How can we go beyond our small limitations and build group consciousness at the same time?)

Create a common goal.
Create a common ideal, purpose, and activity.
Work together to create what you have imaged.
Eat meals together.
Strive to create a situation where each individual gives to each other and the whole.

6

What are the components of group consciousness and how is it created among a group of people?

Caring about others as if they are yourself.
Thinking of others first.
Creating a common goal within all people in the group or community of growth, learning, transformation and building something lasting and permanent.
Common ideal and purpose.
Love for your fellow man.
Love for all mankind.
Always create new ways to give.

7

What is the difference between group consciousness and interconnectedness?

Group consciousness produces a conscious awareness of the individual's connection with everyone in a group. Adding to this awareness produces conscious awareness and later understanding of one's connection and oneness with all creation.

8

What would the world be like if everyone meditated every day?

It would be like everything good that you can imagine. It would be like honey, and mangoes, and apples, and love, and wisdom, and mental concern, and one big family and enlightenment, and LIGHT would be everywhere. Everyone would be your true, best friend and interconnectedness and Oneness would reign supreme.

9

Why do I sometimes have deeper meditations when meditating in a group than doing it when I am alone?

Because others in the group probably go deeper in meditation than you do. Being in the immediate vicinity of those deeper meditators enables you to go deeper into meditation. In other words, it rubs off on you.

In addition, the group thought form is more powerful than the individual thought form, all other things being equal. Each person's mind adds to the group mind and the group thought form of meditation. The stronger thought form of meditation then carries you deeper into meditation.

10

How does meditating help humanity move into the stage in our evolution called spiritual, intuitive man?

Intuitive Man is the sixth stage or root race of humanity. Man means thinker. The thinker uses the mind. Therefore, Intuitive Man is the Mental thinker that uses more than just the conscious mind. Intuitive Man draws upon the Subconscious Mind also. Meditation quickens the meditator's soul growth and spiritual evolution. Some people are more evolved and some are less evolved due to each person's use or lack of use of will and will power and the image making faculty.

When any person progresses and expands their consciousness it helps all of humanity because that person's consciousness affects all the universe beneficially.

11

Can a leader help to cause group consciousness. If so, how?

Yes. A person is the leader because he or she has some awareness or understanding of group consciousness. A true leader thinks of others and is regularly and constantly creating ways to help teach, give to, and aid the others within his or her sphere of influence as well as expanding his or her creation.

Keep in mind

∞   *Sometimes we have a meditation experience beyond where we are as an inspiration and motivation to have that permanently.*

∞   *Hear the total silence and listen to what's beyond that - profound peace & serenity & unity with creation.*

∞   *Move into it & beyond.*

∞   *When you meditate with people who have deepened their consciousness it "rubs off" on you and draws you into their influence.*

∞   *The more the silence the more you'll be able to explore the infinite potential.*

Chapter Eight

The Superconscious Mind

One of my earliest experiences with cosmic consciousness or Superconscious meditation occurred in Kenosha, Wisconsin. I had just created a spiritual center there and it was flourishing. The following meditation was due in part to this expansive creation that I had caused that was of such great service to the people of Wisconsin.

In the meditation I found myself in a room. The room was built on books and the walls were covered with books. Next, I walked down a tunnel which led to another tunnel that was 5 sided. I forged ahead quickly and all of a sudden I fell through the end of the pentagon tunnel into a large place. This place was like a large pit or well that was very wide. I did not fall to the bottom but rather was suspended in space. Next I experienced, while still suspended in mid-air, being everywhere at once. Everything I had ever experienced fit together and made sense. All the Universal Laws fit together and made sense. Past, present, and future came together and I understood it all. I had attained Universal Consciousness and Universal Understanding. I could and did experience everything at once.

Next, I seemed to come out of that state of Universal Consciousness and Universal Knowing and Universal Understanding and I found myself holding onto or being pressed against two long tall book shelves full of books higher than my head. I could not let go. I was screaming or yelling mainly from the power and awesomeness of the experience. It was as if a million volts of electricity were coursing through me. The phrase I AM is the Alpha and the Omega the One who is and who was and who is to come, came into my mind.

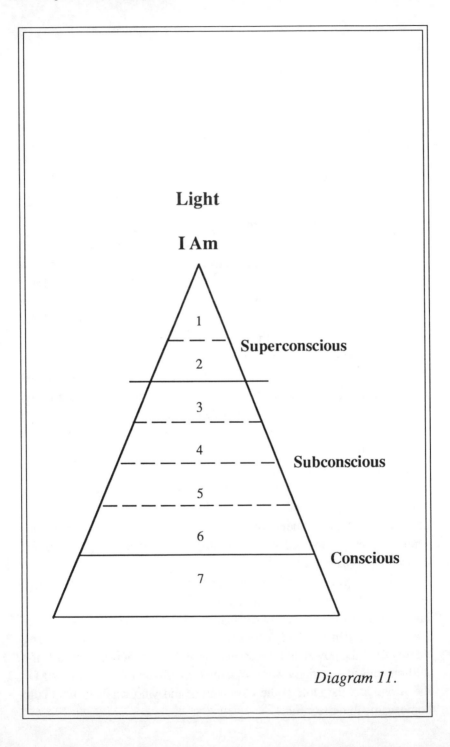

Diagram 11.

Then I seemed to settle down on top of some bookshelves. I realized I had gone beyond most of humanity. I had not let the physical existence trap me in engrossment in the physical senses, karma, and the cycle of reincarnation. I had evolved or moved beyond a type of class or lesson of the physical existence and had passed the test. The test was the test of life to determine if one is to lead a limited physical life, engrossed in the senses or move beyond this type of entrapment.

I realized there were many more tests to come and that I needed to come to understand, wield, and use these tremendous energies for myself and the benefit of humanity.

The division of mind located at the top of the mind chart *(Diagram 11)* is called the Superconscious Mind. Notice its location nearest I AM. This is the division of Mind nearest to your original source as Light.

The Superconscious Mind has as its duty to supply life force to the other divisions of Mind including the Conscious Mind.

The one who experiences cosmic consciousness brings the walls of separation and isolation down and comes to *know* through direct knowledge beyond perception that all of creation is interconnected. Such a one knows that everything done by one person affects all of humanity and, in fact, all of creation. There is direct knowledge and experience of the Universal Laws and Truths and the Universal Principles that cause these laws to function.

It is the Superconscious Mind that those who have developed the Christ or Buddha Consciousness attempt to explain and communicate to others. Unfortunately, up to this point in mankind's history the Universal Language of Mind was known by very few so even when a person experienced Cosmic or Christ consciousness they found it difficult if not impossible to explain to those who had not experienced this expansive consciousness. Parables and stories were used as the best attempt to communicate an idea of what it was like to experience the higher levels of mind.

Metaphors, similes, and analogies were used to communicate to the average person the mysteries of the so-called "kingdom of God" or the abode of the divine. At the same time symbolism was given to the student and initiate at the various levels of growth and awareness.

Superconscious awareness is always associated with an incredible expansion of consciousness. Movement of the attention from Conscious

Mind to Subconscious Mind provides the ability to perceive things in an expansive way that seems like astounding extensions of our five senses. For example, clairvoyance, which means *clear seeing* or *clear viewing*, is the ability to perceive people or events with the mind that are too far away to be seen by ordinary sight. Clairaudience is the ability to hear or perceive with the mind's eye the conversation of a friend many miles distant.

Superconscious awareness is an expansion of one's consciousness much beyond so called psychic abilities. Superconscious awareness is the ability to expand one's awareness and consciousness to all of creation. It is more than the intuitive faculties. It is the experience of the cosmos.

For instance there is a difference between astral projection and expansion of consciousness. Astral projection is the ability to leave one's physical body to move outside of one's body, in full consciousness and travel almost instantaneously, at the speed of thought, to other locations. In the sixth level of Mind one can learn to project outwardly, investigating distant places, far or near that exist in the physical environment. Astral projection beyond the sixth level of Mind to the fifth, fourth, third, second, or first levels of Mind is an inner projection.

At twenty-nine years old, Jay is an entrepreneur in the computer field. He is finding the mind expansion he experiences during meditation encourages innovative thinking in his business. Moreover, it frees him to explore new horizons, venture into virgin territories. Here is one of his favorite meditation experiences that describes the difference between astral projection and the expansion of consciousness.

I was in the countryside on the campus of the College of Metaphysics. I had been chanting the Om for some time when I realized I felt very light. I began to have an experience that I would describe as a unity with all of creation and started to expand my light beyond my body - only I was consciously aware that this was occurring.

This experience lasted a moment and then my attention returned to a "smaller" sphere of consciousness - I was unable to hold this state of consciousness for a very long period of time. But it gave me what I needed to begin understanding myself and others on a deeper level.

OM is the vibration of Creation. Chanting or repeatedly saying OM enables you to more closely identify with your essence which is LIGHT. As consciousness is lifted up and expanded into Superconscious mind you experience oneness with all Creation and everyone in Creation. By being disciplined and committed to meditation every day these expansive experiences become greater and come more often.

Your body, your physical body is the shell, covering, and vehicle you use each lifetime. It is the place the Soul resides while in a physical incarnation. As your light and awareness expand beyond the body you realize you are not limited you are unlimited and the possibilities of what you can achieve with your lifetime are endless. Limitations are only Self imagined.

The further within Mind the projection moves the more the projection is transformed into an expansion of consciousness. In Superconscious Mind the projection is no longer a projection because it requires no movement from one place to another. Rather it requires an expansion of consciousness. An inner projection is the movement of Self in Mind inward to the inner levels of Mind to visit those inner worlds and the inner dimensions of consciousness.

LIGHT is the essence of our being and the movement inward is the motion to gain full understanding of the essence of our being.

1. Prepare your Self for meditation in the usual manner. Sit cross legged on the floor with your back straight. Fill your body with Light. Chant AUM. While chanting AUM direct your Kundalini energy up the center of the spinal column touching and vivifying the seven chakras along the way. Direct the Kundalini energy up to and through the crown chakra located at and directly above the physical head. Perceive your Self as going up through the Mind, through the apex of Superconscious Mind and into I AM and LIGHT. Leave your physical body behind as you expand your consciousness to fill the Universe.

2. Place your attention on your heart chakra or heart center. Perceive a golden ball of Light and Love. Cause it to expand and fill the Universe.

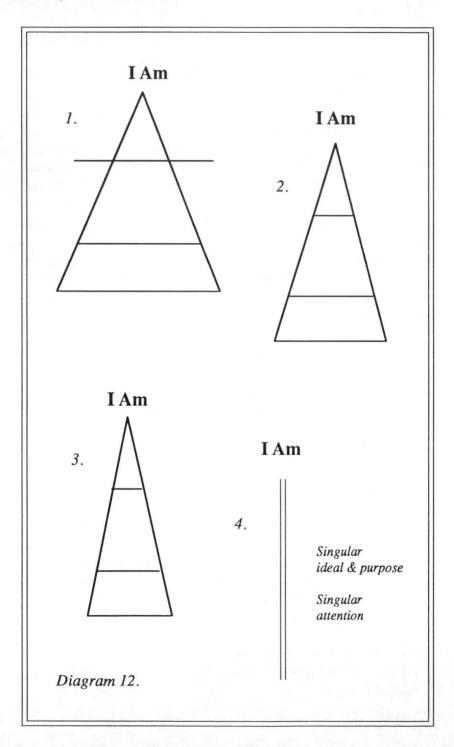

Diagram 12.

In Superconscious Meditation you recognize your kinship with all Creation and everything in it. It is the experience of unity and non-separateness. It is the experience of bliss, love, fulfillment, Light, and peace. It is the experience and the Oneness of non-separation from our Creator. You experience vastness, infinity, and other attributes of the Eternal Creator. After Superconscious Meditation it may take hours, days or weeks to assimilate everything you have received during meditation.

Diagram 12 illustrates what is achieved within the individual when that person has his singular ideal and purpose of life focused on becoming an enlightened individual, a Christ or Buddha, and one who is full of light. The whole attention is on understanding Self and Creation. At this level of evolutionary growth the soul has outgrown the schoolroom we call Mind. All the lessons Mind have to offer have been learned and incorporated into the Self. Therefore, the Real Self moves forward, onward, and upward to the next great level or expanse of creation called The Absolute. A great level of understanding of creation and creatorship has been gained. The Self also understands his or her part in Creation and the Supreme Reality.

Within Superconscious Mind there is no distance or space between minds or individuals as shown by the apex of the Mind triangle diagram. This is why mystics and spiritually enlightened individuals throughout the ages have reported the experience of oneness with all other people and all of creation. Meditation expands the Self to do many things and see many things that are not available to the average person.

In examining the Mind chart again notice that the seventh level of mind, the physical level of Mind or Conscious Mind is pictured as the widest part of the triangle. The Subconscious Mind is pictured as narrower than the Conscious Mind showing the ability to communicate with others on the inner levels of Subconscious Mind over what might physically be termed large distances. Space, time, and distance are creations of the Mind.

The Superconscious Mind is pictured as narrower than the Conscious Mind and even narrower than the Subconscious Mind. At the top of the triangle the dimension of width comes together at a point. This point symbolizes the fact that in Superconscious Mind there is no distance between individuals.

In Superconscious Mind everyone is touching. In Subconscious Mind you are connected with all others but they are at a distance.

In Superconscious Mind we understand that all individuals are all a part of the Divine Creation and everything one person does affects all others. In Superconscious Mind there exists a state of non-separateness. This is why mystics and enlightened individuals have described this experience as Oneness – oneness with all other people and all of creation.

It is not physical time that is important to one in the scope of one's soul progression and evolution. It is the choices that are made and how rich the life is from these choices. Therefore, set your sights on the richness of the experiences and understanding rather than their duration. Finite thinking is not what one is seeking. Awareness and conscious connection with the infinite fulfills the Self.

The more you experience and align with Superconscious Mind the more you think in terms of Universals. Your consciousness stops seeing everything and everyone as separate. You stop seeing the universe as fragmented. Instead you learn to perceive the Universal interconnectedness of all things and all people and all creation. Your consciousness becomes Universal. Your consciousness expands to include more and more of creation. Therefore, you develop omniscience and omnipresence which are all Universal. You also understand Universal communication and the Universal Language of Mind. You enter the cosmic ocean of life, light and love in which all are interconnected. Learn to dwell on the highest plane of truth.

My wife, Barbara, and I often draw upon these attracting, coalescing energies to quicken spiritual evolution, expand our perceptions and re-plenish our spirits. It is perhaps best described in how she talks about the time we devoted to the Parliament of the World's Religions.

The rewards of years of meditation were abundant for
many of the students and faculty of the School of Metaphysics
when we attended the Parliament of the World's Religions the
summer of 1993 in Chicago. Daniel had been invited to give
one of the major addresses on the subject of his then newly-
*released book **Permanent Healing**. Our Interfaith Church of*
Metaphysics choir was performing "The Power of Prayer
throughout the World" and I was to present a seminar on

spiritual initiation. Over 7000 spiritual leaders and aspirants from around the globe had traveled to this Midwestern metropolis for the purpose of bringing mankind together, spiritually.

My consciousness was afire. To be physically connected with people from all over the world who desire spiritual accord was a dream come true. For years I had developed my consciousness inwardly through daily meditation, outwardly through daily teaching and counseling, sometimes in a different U.S. city each day. Through my choices I had expanded my consciousness to include others, all of humanity, in how I think and what I think. Now I had the honor of meeting a global representation of people face to face. The ways the interactions touched my consciousness will live with me forever. Friendships were forged. Realizations came every moment. The intensity of the giving and receiving was awesome.

During Parliament, meditation was when I knew my consciousness could be stilled for an extended time. The daily requirements of responding to needs as they arose was benevolently demanding. And in the context of the spiritual transformation, mental stimulation, emotional excitement, and physical exertion, meditation became my time of restoration and rejuvenation.

Several days into the ten day meeting, the vision of what we were collectively creating was revealed to me during meditation. I was scheduled to give a seminar on "Spiritual Initiation – Gateways to Awareness" the following day. I felt prepared to give but when I awoke around 4 a.m. I found it difficult to get back to sleep. My mind was racing, going over and over the truths I wanted to impart and how I wanted to express them. I decided to seek peace in meditation as this was the best use I could imagine of this unwanted awake time. What happened during that meditation was remarkable, far more meaningful than I had expected.

It was as if I was suspended miles above the surface of a planet. I could see the arcing of the planet surface, so familiar from aerial photographs brought back to us by space travelers.

It seemed like Earth and at the same time not. The vista of what I could see included a large body of water. An island was in the center of my line of sight. Beautiful. Tropical. A paradise bathed in warm sunlight. Off in the distance beyond the island was a shoreline.

When I looked down and back all I could see was the vast darkness of space. When I looked at the waters below, they were turbulent, frothed by winds, seared by lightning. Close-in to the island it was as if an unseen force calmed the waters. At one place the turbulence reigned, at the next the waters were calmed, creating ringlets on the surface that melted into the shore, imperceptible except for the sound of constant lapping of the island sand.

The waters that washed the island shore were quietly transparent. Aquamarine would from this time forward have a new meaning for me. I had never seen such a vibrant, pulsating hue. I still do not believe it exists in our physical world, only within the inner worlds.

Although all of this would have been memorable and meaningful unto itself, what was striking about this meditation was yet to come.

I suddenly realized the concentration of light being showered upon the island. It did not come from a sun, as I would have expected were this occurring in our physical world. Nor was it dispersed from one source like our sun. Rather, the light descended directly upon the island like millions of crystals. They reflected the spectrum, touching everything and everyone with a kind of gold dust, causing them to become iridescent. The image was almost overwhelming. If not for my keenness of curiosity and developed will power I would have lost control of my attention or emotions right then. But I wanted to remain here. I was compelled to stay. I relaxed, easing myself into this beautiful consciousness. I had to know where it came from, and the way to know was to become.

As I forged my consciousness with what I saw, there was a moment of embodying this new realization. It came as if I was standing in the center of this island. I turned my gaze upward

*until I could see directly overhead. The light was all encom-
passing. At that moment it was as if I was transported to a
place of reception, what would be millions of miles above the
planet. A place where light energies from throughout the
darkness were drawn like a magnet. It was unlike anything I
had ever seen before, and something I will always remember.*

*The final image lasted only a moment. It was enough to
sufficiently energize me that I found returning to sleep a
thankless and unnecessary task. I knew I was prepared to give
the best of who I am and what I know later that day. Any outer
anxiety or tension was gone, all remnants of ego reimburse-
ment were cast aside, and I knew I could be a channel for God
when the time came.*

And I was.

*I knew I had achieved a plateau awareness in living
meditatively that had I not chosen to be at this place at this time
I would have missed and perhaps spent years seeking.*

*The memory of my meditation vision came back to me later
that day when we exited the hotel to go home for the night.
This led to a surprising connection to the meditation vision. In
a rush of insight I suddenly realized we were leaving the oasis
of peace, the place of the Parliament. I saw these two floors of
the Palmer House in downtown Chicago as an island. It was
as if it was totally separate from the rest of the world, not only
physically separate but mentally separate. It was an island of
paradise. A place of intense light. Not perfection, for there
were arguments here but nevertheless this conclave was the
closest experience I had ever had, outside of those created by
people in the School of Metaphysics, of people genuinely
caring for each other. Striving to live the universal truths
taught by every religion on this planet since the beginning of
man's sentience. Here people, for the most part, were willing
to listen to each other. They were making sincere efforts to still
their minds and reach that place of communion.*

*It reminded me of many meditation periods in my past.
Where the inner level communion was paradise to the inner
senses; the visions soft, the sounds sweet, the tastes clear, the*

smells still, the touches fresh. Sometimes returning to the density of physical experience was startling, abrasive to my physical senses in the way the smell of exhaust fumes assaulted my nose and the blare of car horns hurt the ears when we left our Parliament paradise. It was like leaving Heaven and entering Sodom and Gommorrah. And few people in Sodom were even aware of the oasis of light existing within their midst. I found myself envisioning how our world will change as the consciousness on those two floors spreads throughout a city, throughout the globe. The prospects are illuminating.

Through the years meditation has helped me realize how much service has been the essence of my life even from childhood, and it has helped me to unravel imagined limitations or egotistical attachments that would taint the beauty in that service. Consciously going within freed me from outer distractions and to serve with my whole Self. More and more, revelations such as these are occurring in my consciousness, enabling me to embody what it means to live meditatively. More and more my consciousness is a continuity of ever-deepening awareness, ever-expanding enlightenment.

And I am so very glad I have remained faithful in my prayer and meditation throughout the years.

All separateness is an illusion and all things are interconnected and whole. This is true within the Self and throughout all of creation. It is our propensity for fragmentation that keeps us from experiencing the intensity of consciousness, joy, love, and delight for existence. Fragmentation or viewing life as separateness always eventually proves destructive. The recognition of the unbroken wholeness of all things can affect changes in the physical body as I explained in detail in my earlier book, *Permanent Healing*.

The purpose of life is to cause a quickening of our soul growth, our soul evolution, and our soul learning. There are two very important steps to this.

1. Learning to love on a deeper and deeper level and on a larger and larger scale because through this love you come to know your connectedness with all beings and all of creation.

2. Permanent understandings which are understanding of Self and Creation. You must gain knowledge of Creation and learn to fully understand all of Creation in order to be like your Creator.

Then you can be a true authority for true authority resides in what one knows. The one who has gained Superconscious awareness has great authority because such a one knows the plan of creation held in Superconscious Mind.

The Superconscious Mind has two parts or levels within it. The first level is the Christ Consciousness or Buddha Consciousness level. The word Buddha is a title meaning *enlightened* or *one who is filled with light*. The word Christ is a Greek word meaning *enlightened* or *anointed* and is the word that was chosen as the translation of the Hebrew word messiah in the Bible when referring to Jesus of Nazareth. Jesus, or Je-Zeus was the Greek word chosen to replace the Hebrew name which is Joshua. Messiah is translated as *anointed*. Christ represents the ideal for humanity which is a definition given in *Webster's New Collegiate Dictionary*.

One who gains the Christ or Buddha Consciousness, the first level of Mind, is filled with the Light of Creation. Such a one's light of awareness has expanded to fill the universe. Having expanded to fill the universe such a one discovers a oneness, unity, interconnectedness, and state of non-separateness between all beings and all of Creation.

Superconscious Mind is the abode or residence of your High Self or spirit just as Subconscious Mind is where your soul resides.

Superconscious Mind is the highest part or division of Mind. It contains the blueprint, plan, or seed idea for you as an individual becoming a whole Self an enlightened Self.

The first level of Mind is the beginning level for the whole Mind. Great souls such as Gautama the Buddha, Jesus of Nazareth, Spitama Zarathustra, Lao Tzu, and Pythagoras (Paterguru) functioned with full awareness in this level of mind and used it effectively for the betterment of mankind.

To gain full awareness and use of the first level of Mind you must first have brought the lower six levels of Mind under control and be using these other levels with conscious awareness.

The Superconsciousness Mind has a kind of complete separation or difference in vibration than the Conscious and Subconscious Mind. This is indicated on the Mind chart by the horizontal line between Subconscious and Superconscious Minds extending beyond the walls of the Mind triangle.

The energies of Subconscious Mind are constantly working to move thought forms and life force into the physical existence. Each level of Mind is receptive to the level of Mind that is immediately higher or beyond itself. For example, the fourth level of Mind is receptive to the third level of Mind and the fifth level of Mind is receptive to the fourth level.

Conversely, each level of Mind is positive to the level immediately below itself. For example, the third level of Mind is aggressive or positive to the fourth level while the fourth level of Mind is positive or aggressive to the fifth level of Mind which is receptive or negative to the fourth level.

The interaction of this aggressive and receptive effect creates a pushing motion as energy and mind substance seeks its lowest level which is ultimately the seventh level of Mind which is commonly referred to as physical existence.

The second level of Mind is called the Causal level or Causal Consciousness. A few people through the ages have learned to expand their consciousness to such a great degree that they are able to achieve conscious awareness and use of this level of Mind. True prophets of ancient times could enter this level of Mind and access the knowledge and wisdom contained therein.

Those who give of their spiritual knowledge to others and have earned their wisdom are gaining the ability to enter this level of Mind. These wise souls encourage, nudge, and draw students to them to learn the inner secrets of Mind so that, they too, may become world servers.

The Superconscious Mind supplies life force or life energy to the Subconscious and Conscious Minds thus enabling humanity to have life in the physical environment. From this gigantic dynamo called Superconscious Mind flows all the power that creates and sustains all the entire creation in the worlds below it.

Those that learn to exist with Superconscious awareness in Superconscious Mind live in a free, infinite, and Universally expansive Higher consciousness of illumination.

The Superconscious Mind, containing both the aggressive and receptive factors of Creation in balance, is complete in itself without dependency on Conscious and Subconscious Mind. However, the Subconscious and Conscious Minds are dependent on the Superconscious Mind both to provide life force and the plan of Creation. Life force from Superconscious Mind makes it possible for I AM to exist in the lower levels or more dense levels of Mind. The perfect seed idea or plan of Creation held in Superconscious Mind is manifested in Subconscious Mind as the individual's soul urge or assignment for a lifetime. In the Conscious Mind it is manifested as the inner drive to achieve desires and goals. In the more developed person this same urge manifests as the ideal and purpose of enlightenment and knowing all of Creation.

The Universal essence of Spirit which is you, the individual, in Superconscious Mind is motion or movement. This motion is the movement from aggressive to receptive to aggressive again. The Aggressive and Receptive Principles of Creation operate continually for Creation operates continually. Creation is eternal. Creation is not a one time event. Creation is continual and eternal. This is why the Creator is eternal.

The secret of life is in forming a complete idea or mental image and causing that image to have consistent and constant motion so that the idea becomes a physical manifestation, a creation, or object in our outer, waking lives.

To fully understand Superconscious Mind you must become a helpmate in the Creator's creation. You must become a world server. The power to do this comes through a still mind. The more you become still in Self the more power you will generate.

The Superconscious Mind contains a balance of both the aggressive and receptive, the positive and negative, factors of Creation. Rhythmic balanced interchanges between all poles of opposite expression is the basis of Creation in this universe of LIGHT. The balanced continuity of aggressive and receptive LIGHT principles in motion is the most fundamental principle of our Holographic Universe.

This perpetually creating electric wave Mind-Universe of two moving Lights or Universal Principles is dynamic and moves forever. It moves from a state of balance to imbalance to balance again, continually.

The foundation of all of Mind and of the entire Universe is stillness, the balanced states of the Aggressive and Receptive principles of Creation in stability, unity, and interconnectedness. Space is not empty, it is full. We exist in a cosmic sea of energy and in the sea of energy we need to interact with the infinite source of our being. In physics the cosmic sea is called the quantum potential field that pervades all space. Its influence does not diminish with distance.

The stillness of the aggressive and receptive, positive and negative principles of Creation in complete balance where all motion has ceased enables one to experience Superconscious awareness. Balance is the key to oneness, interconnectedness, and unity. Once you move beyond Superconscious Mind you have transcended time and space. You realize your immortal nature for you exist in eternity. Therefore, become one continuous effort toward enlightenment.

In highest meditation you go beyond Mind to eternal joy, eternal wisdom, eternal peace, eternal LIGHT, and eternal love. You become steeped in bliss. You have uninterrupted communion with the Supreme.

Time, space, and distance are a function of Mind. We exist in Mind. We also exist in the physical universe which is the level of Mind farthest away from LIGHT and Superconscious Mind. The farther you are from LIGHT the more you and the rest of humanity experience the scattering effect of Mind. The substance of Mind vibrates at a slower rate becoming physical substance or objects. This leads to the misguided thinking that everything is separate including yourself. This separatist thinking in turn leads to loneliness. It also leads to scientific materialism which views everything as separate and dead when in fact, the universe is alive. The slowing down of the rate of vibration of Mind substance in order to form our physical environment creates a condition where the results of our causal thoughts and attitudes often take some time to return to us. This time lapse leads to a situation where it is difficult to perceive a cause-effect relationship.

The Mayans understood vertical time. They measured time in a way that was in alignment with Subconscious and Superconscious Mind. The western world measures time horizontally which is limited to a physical measurement without regard to the rest of Mind.

Space is a function of distance. While time is a function of the movement between two separate objects that are separated by distance. By looking at the Mind chart provided in this book you can see that the deeper or higher into Mind your consciousness expands the less distance there is between anything whether it be souls or Mind Substance. Time and distance function less and less the deeper into Mind you go. Interconnectedness replaces time and distance. It has taken me 20 years of meditation to discover this and much of what is in this book.

Engrossment in a physical body creates the illusion of being separate and alone. The deeper into Mind, the higher into Mind one moves the less separateness, aloneness, and selfishness there is. When this is realized there is no longer the need to become attached to people, places, and things for they are always with you. All points in space become equal to all other points in space and it is meaningless to speak of anything as being separate from anything. Quantum physics calls this property nonlocality. Nonlocality equals, "we are all one."

The final two stages of enlightenment carry you beyond the Superconscious Mind. The essence or spirit that is you goes beyond all of Mind to first I AM and then LIGHT.

When you expand your consciousness beyond the vehicle of experience called Mind you first experience, I AM. In the teachings of India this is called Nirvikalpa samadhi. Nirvikalpa samadhi is referred to as a state in which the embodied soul realizes its unity with the Absolute.

The final stage in earthly evolution is the expansion of consciousness beyond Mind and beyond I AM to the full experience, awareness, knowing, and understanding of LIGHT. The meditators of India call this state Mahasamadhi which is total absorption from which the mind and soul never returns to physical existence. The experience of LIGHT does not mean you lose your individuality or identity. Instead it is the Universal awareness and consciousness of your interconnectedness with all beings, all of the Creator's Creation and the Creator. You are no longer separate and life is not fragmented to your perceptions. You fully perceive the Universe as alive and all as part of one whole Creation with all affecting everyone and everything else in Creation.

I don't remember when I experienced my greatest medita-
tion, but I experienced an expression of love for creation.
During my meditation I experienced much joy. It was like
basking in a ray of sunlight, in alignment with God. The joy
filled my being. I was in an expanded awareness. A message
came in a knowing sense. I meditated on the secrets of creation

*and they opened to me. Each time I was getting closer to God
and creation.*
*This meditation experience was a source of inspiration.
Each meditation period I want to learn what God knows to help
me manifest the things I desire.*

Meditation carries you to a higher light. The Light of awareness and understanding. Meditation carries you closer to God. Meditation carries you closer to the source of your creation. The greater your alignment within your Self the greater your alignment with the Eternal Creator. The greater your stillness of mind the more you will experience a ray of sunlight until the ray expands to fill you full of Light. Your life will then be full of Light, understanding, awareness, and en-light-en-ment. You will always receive the message you need to know. You will then always receive the answer to your sincere, and earnest prayers. You will know your purpose in life and your life will have greater meaning leaving you with a deep and fulfilling satisfaction.

The greatest step, the final word, the end result of the greatest realization is to have the High Consciousness be with the Supreme, Eternal, Creator in all living beings of the world with full Conscious awareness. The Highest form of meditation is when one is in a state of singleness always.

1

Where is the Superconscious Mind?

Everywhere.

2

What is the Superconscious Mind?

The abode of the Spirit, the High Self, which is your own individual superconscious mind.

3

What is the duty of the Superconscious Mind?

To provide life force to all of Mind.

4

What is the purpose of Superconscious Mind?

To hold the blueprint for all creation including the plan for you becoming a whole functioning Self.

5

What is the first level of Mind?

It is the highest level of Mind and is called Christ Consciousness.

6

What is the second level of Mind?

The second level of Mind is called the Causal level.

7

What exists in Superconscious Mind?

The plan for all Creation. The first and second level of Mind.

8

To become enlightened is it necessary to experience the Superconscious Mind?

The two go hand in hand. There is no difference.

9

Why is the Superconscious Mind depicted in many texts as a Tao symbol, a yin-yang symbol?

The Superconscious Mind holds and is a balance of the Aggressive and Receptive Principles of Creation.

10

What is the relationship between God and Superconscious Mind?

The Superconscious Mind is the Holy of Holies where God may be realized. In Superconscious meditation the physical body is left behind. The consciousness of the meditator expands to fill all of creation. You are meditating not only for yourself but for all humanity.

In Superconscious meditation you, the meditator, experience bliss. The meditator who has held within the attention an image of Light is now filled with LIGHT. The meditator may experience a desire to stay or remain in meditation rather than return to the physical existence. This thought or desire must be overcome for it is just such a one that has much to offer humanity. Everyone's inner urge is to move forward to the LIGHT of Awareness and Self understanding. Such a meditator acts as a beacon of Light for all others to move toward so they may safely reach the shores of their own understanding and Enlightenment.

The goal of humanity is for everyone to be enlightened. The enlightened meditator, the Superconscious Meditator can be and is of tremendous service towards this goal. The Superconscious meditator is of more use to humanity in this regard than all the world's politicians put together because such a one is already living the future of humanity.

The future of humanity is enlightenment. The future of humanity is God consciousness and alignment with all creation. The Superconscious meditator is living the future now and thereby drawing others into the future with him. He is also accelerating mankind's growth into its true and expected future according to Divine Plan.

The Divine Plan is for everyone to know creation and be enlightened and therefore, reach a level of compatibility with our Creator. We thereby become creators in our own right and a help-mate in creation.

Long before the meditator has achieved Superconscious meditation he or she has recognized the need for Self to be a server of mankind, a world server. In order to expand your consciousness to all humanity and all of Mind you must first serve humanity.

A world server understands the Laws of Creation. He teaches these Universal Laws of Mind to his inner circle of students and they in turn teach it to others. They work diligently to aid in the uplifting of humanity in order that we may all progress into a state of God Consciousness. By so doing the Enlightened One eliminates countless millennia of sorrow and lifetimes of pain for not only Self but for others to the degree they are willing to serve. The greatest Masters of Consciousness throughout history have been world servers. They have not been businessmen. The Superconscious meditator is filled with LIGHT. He or she has a love for humanity as a loving father has for his children who are immature yet have the capacity and potential to grow up and be compatible with their maker.

From meditation in the first and second levels of consciousness you will receive freedom, joy, bliss, and the peace that goes beyond all physical, conscious mind understanding.

When you experience fully beyond Superconscious Mind to I AM and LIGHT you may experience total fulfillment, joy, bliss, happiness, total knowledge, and total love.

A business partner with her husband, a mother of a ten-year-old daughter who she home schools, and a spiritual teacher and director of a School of Metaphysics center, Teresa has a full and satisfying life. She attributes much of the true success of her life to daily meditation, for meditation has brought her the confidence and security to respect who she is and move toward her dreams.

The greatest meditation I've had thus far occurred after I had been meditating on the question of, "What is my purpose in life?" I had meditated on this question for what seemed like a month. Then one day, before I sat down to meditate I knew that I was going to receive my answer. Looking back I now know I was finally receptive. I was ready to receive my answer.

So once again, I stated my question and then proceeded to meditate. In the middle of my meditation, I felt a rush of energy come into my whole being. It felt like a hot flash or the feeling you get right before you're about ready to plunge forward off the edge of a rollercoaster. I became very warm, full of light, uplifted and light, as if a part of myself had just dropped off, that is a part of my body had just been left behind.

I was enormously free! Then I saw a vision of Mother Teresa. I heard the words, "You are the chosen one". Then I heard and felt and I think experienced throughout my whole being "love". After this wonderful experience, I knew the chosen one to be that of love.

The first creation of the Creator was light. Once an idea has been thought of and created in the mind's eye it is necessary to shine the light of attention on it. The light of attention is awareness. After this first creation of Light the Creator created individualized units of LIGHT called I AM. Each individualized unit of LIGHT was and is an I AM. I AM began experiencing in first the Superconscious Mind then Subconscious Mind and finally in the Conscious Mind also known as the physical existence.

So at the core of each person's being is light. LIGHT is our essence. We were made from LIGHT and LIGHT we are. Teresa asked the question, "What is my purpose in life?" Through perserverence she received the answer to her question in meditation. You need to always be receptive in meditation. Teresa became full of light in answer to her question. She was uplifted as her attention moved higher into Mind and her consciousness expanded. She experienced freedom because she was no longer limited by her physical body and the five senses. When your consciousness is able to expand to encompass the world you are free for you have freedom of awareness and freedom of motion and freedom to create and freedom to be everything you are meant to be.

Love is the glue that binds all of creation together. Every I AM, every person was created out of an act of love by our Creator. Love is embedded in all of Creation. It is our work to dis-cover and un-cover this love. It is our duty to stop closing off to this love and to open completely to this love. The Creator chose love as his modus operandi for transmitting and making the LIGHT of Creation available to all people and all beings of creation. Yes, the chosen one is Love.

In Superconscious Mind there is not motion as we think of motion in our physical existence. In the physical environment we experience everything as separate from ourselves therefore, we must travel from where we are to the location of another person in order to be with them. In Superconscious Mind we are not separated by distance, which is space. In Superconscious Mind we are already connected with all other beings and all of Creation. Therefore, we do not need motion to go to the location of another. Neither do we need time because we can be instantly where another is by aligning our consciousness with the other person.

Time is an expression of distance or space. In Superconscious Mind space is compacted and distance between individuals ceases to exist. For example, watch the second hand of a clock. A minute is the amount of time required for the second hand to traverse the distance around the face of a clock. The same is true for the minute hand which must go completely around the face of a clock in an hour. The same is true for a day which we measure by the time it takes the sun to traverse the sky and return to its original position. So you see even time is relative to distance in our perception. Take away space or distance and time becomes endless or eternal. We become timeless.

1

What is the highest level of meditation?

Direct communion with the Creator-Eternal-Supreme.

2

Can the Superconscious Mind be accessed by the waking, conscious mind with directed effort and will?

No but it can be achieved with conscious awareness. The conscious mind is associated with the physical body.

3

Is it possible to astral project into the Superconscious division of Mind?

You must receive Superconscious Mind not aggressively force yourself in.

4

What quality of thinking can I practice to heighten my mind to receive Superconscious awareness?

Learn to receive. Let your walls of protection come down and learn to receive. Open the door and let all of creation in and enter into your innermost being. All of creation means all that is good and productive and adds to the evolution of mankind, the planet, and the entire universe for truly we are connected with everything in creation.

Everything we do affects everything else in creation. Practice listening at all times.

5

How do I know I am receiving from Superconscious Mind rather than my subconscious or conscious mind?

You will change and grow and become more enlightened every day. Your habits will no longer control you. Your consciousness will be uplifted. You will recognize your oneness with all creation and the interconnectedness of all things. It will be more than an intellectual concept. You will know.

6

How can I connect with my own Superconscious Mind?

Still and quiet the mind. Scattered conscious thoughts are of the conscious mind which is of the physical existence. To receive the higher Mind you must quiet your thoughts and still the mind.

7

Sometimes I am really light headed after meditating. Why and what can I do different?

Do nothing different. You feel light headed because your consciousness has been lifted up to the higher reaches of the mind. After awhile, as you learn to apply and use this higher consciousness in your waking life you will find it is natural and you will yearn for his experience.

8

As my meditation deepens daily and over years, what kind of effects or benefits can I look forward to?

Increased peace and fulfillment with yourself and your life. Greater service to mankind. Greater understanding of all creation and of everything in the world and everything in your life. The increased ability to create and have your life as you desire it to be, productive, fulfilling, and full of love.

9

How can I exist with awareness in Superconscious Mind and be actively involved with my daily activities such as teaching and lecturing?

Always maintain a quiet mind and think of others first as if they are a part of yourself.

10

Where does the Light come from during meditation?

The LIGHT of Awareness in Superconscious Mind.

Chapter Nine

Kundalini

In order to truly understand the meditation process an awareness of the Kundalini energy and its process is needed.

You have been told that it is important for the back and spine to be straight and erect during meditation. I also gave you instruction to hold your head balanced on top of the spine without tilting either forward or backward during meditation. Now here is a deeper reason for this position in meditation. It allows the Kundalini energy to move up the spine and out through the crown of the head.

What is Kundalini energy? The word Kundalini is a word from India that means literally *Serpent Fire*. What is the Serpent Fire or Kundalini? The Kundalini is a creative energy that resides at the base of the spine in every individual. In the normal, or average person, this energy is dormant and resides in a coiled up form much like the shape of a snake in a coiled up circle.

As the individual becomes enlightened this energy is aroused. Then the Kundalini energy rises up the spine through the chakra and finally out the crown of the head. When this is achieved the soul has reached true enlightenment.

Throughout history there have been a few individuals who have achieved the full enlightenment. Of these few only a small portion have been recorded by history so that we know of them today. Some of these enlightened individuals known to history are Joshua the Messiah by the Greek version of his Hebrew name, Jesus who became the Christ or Je-Zeus the Cristos, Guatama who became the Buddha, Spitama Zarathustra who is also called by the Greek version of his title Zoroaster, Pythagorus or Pater (Father) Guru, Lao-Tzu, Appolonius of Tyana, Thrice Greatest Hermes, and Mani. Other possible examples of enlightenment are Muhammed, Confucius, Elijah, Moses, Ramakrishna, Swedenborg, Gandhi, Guru Nanak and many others history has failed to note.

When a person begins meditation their whole consciousness begins to change. Since the consciousness of the individual shapes and forms the physical body the body begins to change also. The physical body becomes more refined and closely aligned with light. The three channels in the center of the spine, the Ida, the Pingala, and the Shushumna open, allowing the Kundalini to pass through and up the spine.

The base of the spine is aligned with the gross or physical person. The person that is engrossed in the five senses and sensory experiences has no experience with Kundalini. This is because the Serpent Fire or Kundalini is a mental energy that rises in the physical body. It takes a mental or spiritual being not an intellectual to arouse this mental energy. Until the mind, body, and consciousness become spiritualized the Kundalini remains dormant.

The Kundalini, therefore, has it own built-in safety mechanism. For to be able to have access to this tremendous energy in its full form the individual must first become spiritualized and operate from there through the spleen chakra, to the solar plexus or navel chakra to the heart chakra, to the throat chakra, to the brow chakra and finally, perhaps most importantly, to and through the crown chakra located at the top of the head and above it.

When the Kundalini energy moves up and into the crown chakra, Cosmic or Universal consciousness is achieved. The soul enters the physical body and manifests its consciousness and life force through the seven ductless glands associated with the inner level energy transformers.

The spine needs to be straight because this is the channel the seven centers of LIGHT are able to utilize. This is also the channel the Kundalini energy uses to move from its abode at the base of the spine. The spinal cord becomes a tube. The Kundalini faces up this tube in the spine all the way to the point between the eyebrows known as the third eye or the pituitary gland and finally up and through the crown chakra located at and above the top of the head. Along the way the Kundalini quickens and enlivens the seven energy transformers known as the chakras.

This is illustrated in one of Sharka's meditations. Born in Czechoslovakia fifty-two years ago, Sharka has spent half her life in the United States. She began meditating as part of her study in the School of Metaphysics, reaching the third and final level of study known as the Adam lessons. Here she describes a meditation experience which reflects a quickening of awareness directly linked to the chakras and the Kundalini.

My most exciting meditation was last night. I asked God to fill me with his presence. I experienced energy from my crown chakra meeting with the energy coming from my feet. I felt the presence of God and then I realized that I was that presence. I was very alert and I experienced seeing light. After the meditation I didn't even want to sleep. Although, I was tired after working the whole day.

Before each meditation you need to formulate a prayer, a petition, a request, or question that you want answered. Sharka gave the highest request and this is what she received. The Creator, Eternal, Supreme is always present and available to us. What is required to experience God is an open heart, and an overwhelming desire and need to know God. Light symbolizes awareness and God is the Supreme awareness. There is no end to perception and higher awareness. This is the meaning of the meditator being alert after the meditation.

The crown chakra has been referred to in Indian literature as the thousand petaled lotus. Chakra is a Sanskrit word meaning *wheel*. The chakras are round vortexes that transmit and transform energy. They have spokes or division lines radiating from their center. The chakras' purpose is to recycle used energy back into the inner levels of Mind where it can be processed, re-vitalized, and made ready for further manifestations on the part of the thinker.

As the person learns to meditate the chakra quickens the rate of spinning. As the meditator progresses and enters deeper and deeper levels of meditation learning to apply the meditative experience in the daily life, the speed of rotation of the chakras increases even more. When the spiritualized thinker draws many others to the Self to teach the deep secrets of meditation while continuing to deepen his own meditation and apply it in the life there comes a time when the chakras reverse. This is because no longer does the mental energy of the spiritualized being need to be recycled into mind for all energy is now being used completely in the physical existence. All thoughts, manifestations, and creations are being used fully for enlightenment and the benefit of all mankind. Therefore, there is nothing to recycle.

Sometimes the chakras are stimulated into greater action by the strong desire and imagination of a person. The result is usually but not always temporary. Years ago before I began meditating in a daily disciplined way, I experienced a golden ball of light, a golden sun bursting out of my chest and out of my body. Immediately following this I was in astral projection. This experience was definitely a result of the Kundalini being raised from the base of my spine all the way up to my heart chakra. This was from my desire and efforts to astral project and to experience consciously the inner levels of mind. This is why the energy always seemed so powerful. This was a result of my sincere desire and effort toward soul growth and spiritual development.

Terry also experienced the heart chakra energies during meditation. Here is one of her most profound experiences.

A time when I was very much at peace, as if time stood still.
There was a presence behind me, some energy. It was as if it
entered my body through my heart and expanded filling my
entire being with pure love. I could have stayed there forever.

One of the most powerful things a person can experience is love. The other things are light and peace. Our universe was and is created from an act of love. Love creates, love builds and love grows. Love may be experienced anywhere and it may be experienced throughout the physical body. Love is centered in the heart. Pure love issues from the heart and in a highly developed entity love from the heart is experienced by all in his or her environment.

Once one has experienced pure and full love that person never forgets it. They love to experience that love again and they long to make that love a part of themselves. This type of love will overpower anything. This is the love that all are destined to become, sooner or later, depending on the individual and how quickly they choose to progress.

The meditative experience I earlier described in this book of going down a tunnel, being suspended in space, the abyss, and experiencing past, present, and future and all of Creation and all the Universal Laws and Universal Truths and receiving a million volts of electricity was definitely a result of raising the kundalini up and through my chakras.

As mankind evolves from the Root Race known as Reasoning Man to the next Root Race known as Intuitive Man, more and more individuals will experience the raising of the Kundalini energy to various degrees. More and more people will recognize the reality of the Kundalini from direct personal experience rather than it lying dormant at the base of the spine where few people are aware of the Kundalini and its awesome potential.

Kundalini is aroused from its slumber in a safe, natural, and normal way by the use of meditation. Meditation is beneficial in a universal manner. Through meditation, only when you are ready to receive and use more creativity, imagination, desire, and will shall more Kundalini energy be made available to you.

Since Kundalini energy is creative energy it is necessary to master one's physical existence through one's creative abilities. As you learn to apply the meditative experience in your daily life to create your life the way you desire it to be and the way it needs to be for maximum soul growth a growing awareness of how to wield the Kundalini energy occurs within the individual. As the Kundalini energy rises up the spine it stimulates the highest points of awareness within the individual which is referred to as the crown chakra. Once an individual has reached this heightened state of awareness it does not require a great deal of physical preparation to reach a heightened state of meditation.

Animals do not have chakras or Kundalini energy. Animals have tails which ground them and their energy in the physical existence. People do not normally have tails. This is because the evolutionary impulse of man is to be no longer grounded in the physical but to move and evolve upward to a higher consciousness.

The Kundalini energy has been known by all cultures throughout history under various names. In ancient mythology there is usually a god that symbolizes or represents Kundalini. Kundalini has sometimes been referred to as the spirit fire in western religion or western civilization. A snake in mythology and in Holy Books refers to the Kundalini. Moses led the tribes of Israel out of Egypt by raising the brazen serpent in the wilderness. Moses turned his staff into a snake that devoured the staffs of Pharaoh's priests that they had turned into snakes in the book of *Genesis* of the <u>Bible</u>. In the book of *Revelation* the ancient serpent is the Kundalini that has grown and been aroused as mankind has evolved. The "seven churches of Asia" in *Revelation* represent the seven chakras that are

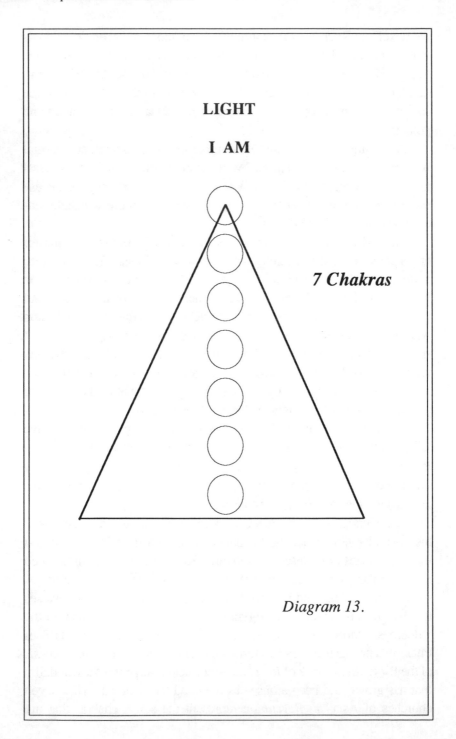

LIGHT

I AM

7 Chakras

Diagram 13.

stimulated to greater activity as the Kundalini creative energy is aroused. The time between *Genesis* and *Revelation* in the Bible symbolizes the evolution of the thinker from the beginnings of Reasoning Man to the Completion of Intuitive Man.

Quetzalcoatl was one of the most remarkable of the crucified world saviors. He was a savior to the Mayans of the Yucatan of southern Mexico and Guatemala. This immortal whose name means *feathered snake* came out of the sea bearing a mysterious cross. The snake symbolizes the Kundalini energy.

The caduceus emblem of the physician is a symbol of the Kundalini. The staff represents the spinal column. The two snakes are the Ida and Pingala, the receptive and aggressive energies of creation. The middle channel of the spine is utilized by the Sushumna power which is the Kundalini rising.

In time, as the meditator has learned to calm the body, still his mind, enter the silence – all at will – impressions from the highest levels of mind will make themselves known. Sometimes, as Dr. Al's experience exemplifies, meditations will convey great spiritual messages of mythic proportions.

> *My body, clothed in brown earthen-colored clothing, was crawling on the ground. A quiet stream was flowing through the land.*
>
> *Then I was in a small wooden boat slowly and silently gliding along. All was calm and peaceful. An alligator-like reptile, which turned into a snake, was rising up. A wide stream of orange light poured upward in a glowing vibratory pattern. "Thy Kingdom come," as it is told in the Lord's Prayer.*
>
> *A song, having the simple words, "Hallelujah Lord," all in the silence.*

Al is 75 years young. He has been meditating for several years. Even though he had never meditated before entering the School of Metaphysics he was able to learn to meditate at the age of 65. He has been more disciplined with his daily practice of meditation than some people I have seen that are half his age. The prayer or petition presented to the inner mind concerned understanding the love of giving. An answer to this question came then in meditation.

Anyone, at any time, can learn to find answers to their questions by using meditation. Dr. Al was able to apply this newfound awareness in his daily life. In order for meditation to be used properly the meditator must know how to apply the new awareness gained from meditation in his daily life. If it is not immediately put into practice, it becomes just a temporary realization, fading like short term memory. When the knowledge is immediately used in the life to benefit Self and others over time the new awareness can be built into a permanent understanding that will be with you always throughout eternity. Build enough understandings and you gain enlightenment.

You are never too old for meditation and the insights it brings, nor are you ever too young. Crystal began meditating at the end of her teenage years, not long after puberty. Puberty is a physical sign that the consciousness has changed, for the Kundalini energies have been genetically awakened. It is common among those experiencing puberty and the teenage years for there to be an acute awareness of the explosion of creative energies within them.

My best meditation experiences usually include a sense of joy and elation, calmness, a separation from my body, and feeling the Kundalini rising up my spine. I have on a couple occasions experienced my Kundalini rising and seeing light bursting from my head. If I had to choose one, however, I would have to choose the meditation I had about a month ago, because of the awareness it brought to me.

I was meditating on my assignment and became aware that I needed to shine and embrace the inner part of me that desires to be important since I had been pushing that part of me away. It felt great to embrace that thought.

The challenge of an awakened Kundalini is to direct those energies toward spiritual enlightenment, mental procreation. As Crystal was beginning to learn an active Kundalini demands an evaluation of who and what is important. The consciousness must change, it must evolve. The aware use of the universal law of proper perspective brings fulfillment. It nourishes the soul.

Kundalini is creative energy. It rests at the base of the spine. When an individual has reached the point in their soul growth where they are ready to experience a glimpse of the mighty creative power within the self, the Kundalini awakes from its slumber at the base of the spine and rises up the spine and out the crown of the head. This experience tells the individual that they need to give their whole attention to knowing the Self. Distractions from this ideal should be eliminated as soon as possible.

Remember, you need other people to create with in order to learn to be a creator. Therefore all that you learn and gain in the way of understanding of the Self and Mind is to be taught and given to others with like desires and willingness to learn and grow.

In this way we live meditatively, individually, collectively, and universally. We grow closer to our Creator because we understand more fully what it means to create with thought.

1

When this light is rising up my spine preceding medita-
tion, is this supposed to be the Kundalini energy?

Yes.

2

How can I cause my Kundalini to raise in meditation?
Does this have a specific transforming effect?

You may visualize or image the Kundalini energy rising
up the spine while willing it to do so. You may contract
the buttocks as a physical aid to stimulating the Kundalini
to rise. You may image yourself as being like the great
enlightened individuals of the past and present.

3

Why are the chakras considered the third stage of
meditation?

Because you first need to learn to still your mind and
remove your attention from your physical body.

4

What is the role of Kundalini in reaching enlighten-
ment?

It is the way that a mental energy that is experienced
and manifested in the physical existence can be aroused,
transformed, and lifted up with the consciousness of the
individual.

5

How may I carry the bliss of meditation with me into my daily life?

When you come out of meditation strive to maintain the blissful, high consciousness experience for as long as you can instead of jumping up with a start and rushing off to do something physical. Remember what that consciousness feels like, looks like, smells like, and sounds like. Be that consciousness.

6

I have seen statues of Buddhas and pictures of Hindu gods or goddesses that are meditating with their hands in the position we use for Kundalini projection. What is the purpose of the hand position with the first two fingers touching the thumb and can it be used to meditate?

These statues represent one who has gained enlightenment. Such a one has full control, understanding of, direction and use of the Kundalini or Creative energy. Such a one is a creator. For such a one the whole life is meditation whether sitting, walking, standing, running, or playing. For such a one is constantly giving to all humanity. Such a one has world consciousness. The statues indicate all this and more.

7.

What is the tingling sensation that fills my body after a deep meditation?

This is the tingling energy of higher consciousness and has moved into and permeated your entire being raising your vibration. You are now more alive for it is the tingling of life all the way to your nerve endings. Strive to have and maintain this higher vibration at all times for it means you are closer to Cosmic Consciousness.

8.

On rare occasions I have received or generated a phrase or idea that sent a shock wave through my body, and I would either physically tingle, shake, shiver, grin, cry, laugh, or speak nonsense. Does this just mean I had a shallow meditation and was not in control of my emotions, or is it something else?

It means you received the answer to your prayers in the form of an idea from the inner levels of mind and your physical consciousness was not evolved enough to receive the new, expanded idea easily. Strive to expand your consciousness and the ability to receive. You need to teach others what you are learning so you may learn how to translate, interpret, and communicate your inner level experiences. You also need to learn the Universal Language of Mind.

9.

Why do I feel like energies are coursing through my body during different stages of meditation, i.e. 15 minutes, then 30 minutes in, I feel waves of energy?

Because they are. Learn to use these greater and higher energies for the benefit of mankind. They are the energies of life and higher consciousness.

10.

I have been meditating for several years and have noticed a gradual deepening of my meditations. At times there are insights and revelations that seem to go way beyond my normal consciousness. I have wondered why these glimpses of the divine seem so unpredictable and how I might experience them all the time in my meditations?

They are so unpredictable because you haven't yet earned that higher level of consciousness. The soul in its infinite joy and compassion desires to give you glimpses of what you may become and what you may permanently have by continuing with what you have begun. It is a stimulus to reach higher and to double your efforts to make the Cosmic Consciousness a permanent understanding full and complete within yourself. Give to the world freely what you are gaining and learning.

Chapter Ten

Completion

On special occasions, when there is a common ideal in our consciousness, students and faculty here at the College of Metaphysics gather together for chanting and meditation. Sometimes these invoke deep states of realization, at others they provoke enlightening instruction and discussion.

I have noticed a tendency for people when instructed to come out of meditative states with the words, "Take a deep breath and open your eyes," to immediately jerk, to fitfully move around, as though they are in a hurry. Meditation is not something that you need to be or want to be "out of" in a hurry. Just like you don't hurry to get into meditation, you don't hurry to get out of meditation. Your goal is to carry that meditation experience – that vibration, energy, alignment, intuition, perception, illumination – with you throughout the day, sharing and giving to all with whom you come in contact, and even all those you don't, for you are connected to the whole world. This is how meditation reaches its fruition.

It is important then to think of meditation as a way of thinking, a way of living. This realization comes in time and is a result of regular, daily meditation periods. At some point the realization arrives that meditation, rather than something apart from your life, a time you set aside each day to commune with God, is the heart, the soul, of your life. You understand meditation is a way to be connected with all of life throughout the day.

Following meditation I often experience a buzzing, a tingling, a vibration going on in my head. When you hurriedly jerk your consciousness out of meditation, bringing all of your attention back to the five senses and your consciousness outward into the physical you miss this afterglow. The realities of meditation are something you want to bring with you. One of the ways you first experience this is through memory. Recalling often the love, warmth, comfort, joy, security, freshness, freedom of the morning's meditation changes the way you view the people and situations throughout the day. It is similar to the magic that seems to occur when we are in love. It is not only the person we hold in high affection who benefits from the constant supply of loving energy that fills us; everyone we meet basks in its glow. And so it becomes with meditation.

The following is a statement of the movement of consciousness following a group meditation led by myself. Also included are questions students asked me after the group meditation and my answers to those questions.

"In time awareness grows to encompass the dimensional realities of meditation. For instance the vibration I note following meditation is the movement of cosmic energies through my consciousness and into my body. The energy from my meditation moves from the Universal Consciousness down to the Crown of my head. It moves from there to my third eye, that is physically the pituitary gland or the point between the eyebrows.

"I can and am experiencing this movement of energy and consciousness right now. This is where the energy and consciousness are residing now. My attention is being drawn out more and more into the physical existence. This is the process I am experiencing now."

Student: Has it taken that long for the energy to go back to your physical body?

"Had I chosen to, I could have jumped around very quickly and wiggled and shook my body and in the process brought my attention fully out into the physical immediately after meditation. This is not what I choose to do with my mind, my consciousness and my attention. I want to and choose to continue to experience my higher level of meditation and higher level of consciousness throughout an extended period of time. I also choose for this higher consciousness to be extended for longer and longer periods of time throughout the day. Thereby, my whole life can be a meditation and I can exist in constant meditation."

Student: After I meditate I sometimes feel sleepy. Is it normal to feel sleepy immediately after meditation?

"I don't feel sleepy now. I feel very refreshed. I feel very invigorated. I feel relaxed. The muscles and nerves along my spine and back are still tingling. I feel very peaceful. It is easy to go sleep after meditation because of all of those reasons.

"There is a tendency for the undisciplined mind to want to go to sleep during meditation, when you are trying to meditate and immediately after meditation. This is because of the fact that before the student learns to discipline the mind the conscious mind knows two states of being: One state is the condition of being awake in the conscious mind and absorbed in the five senses. The second state is that condition we call sleep in which the conscious mind has shut down and the attention of the individual has moved into Subconscious Mind without control.

"When you begin to meditate you close your eyes and you notice you are no longer receiving sensory stimulation from the eyes which is where the normal person receives most of their perceptions from. You also notice you do not taste anything, you don't smell much of anything and you don't feel or touch much of anything because you are sitting there quietly and very still. After awhile you don't even notice the body itches any more and your conscious mind registers the outside noises less and less. As you go deeper and deeper in meditation you don't even notice the physical environment at all.

"As a result of this the physical body rebels. It says, 'Now wait a minute. I'm supposed to be awake, experiencing the five senses.' The conscious mind joins in and agrees with the physical body. The conscious mind may say to you, 'I'm supposed to be shut down and asleep.' Then the physical body and conscious mind try to go to sleep. During sleep your conscious mind is turned off or shut down and your attention goes to the Subconscious Mind.

"But that's not what we want. We want to maintain conscious awareness to learn to transfer your conscious awareness into Subconscious Mind, and deeper and deeper levels of Mind. So the resistance to discipline is a normal way of the conscious mind attempting to be habitual, which you do not want to occur. It is best if you don't go into sleep immediately after meditation, especially until you've mastered the conscious mind.

"Was there anyone else whose meditation is under 45 minutes? Okay, Paul? Thirty minutes? And what did you experience after 30 minutes?

Student: I noticed that there was a cycle in my meditation that at 30 minutes I found myself more back and aware of the physical more.

Student: That somehow I knew that it was time to come back.

Student: And then I realized, Well, we're going to be continuing, so I just started a new cycle.

Student: And then to keep up that mastery, you have to practice.

"That's true."

Student: Like anything.

"Right."

Student: So, is there a point where you get to —first of all, I guess the first question would be you master the conscious mind, and then it is simply a matter of keeping it disciplined?

"There is a point, as I've been explaining to you, and showing to you in describing my experience of meditation where meditation becomes more and more part of your life. In fact, from the very start, you should attempt to and begin to implement your meditation—your meditative experience more and more in your life. As it becomes more and more of your life, there will come a time when experiences in your life are a type of meditation. When you gain a mastery of meditation then life becomes a meditation – one long meditation because there is full alignment of conscious, subconscious, and superconscious minds at all times.

"Now my attention has moved further out into my physical body so my feet want to feel the carpet. My feet want to feel the carpet because I allow my attention to move all of the way back into the physical existence. The carpet feels good on my feet. My feet want to feel that sensory experience and I am letting them do that now but it has been 20 minutes since we finished meditation and 20 minutes before I allow my feet to have this sensory experience although they would have liked to much sooner. This is because the physical body is like an animal and therefore, desires immediate sensory gratification.

"Over time you will find that that you will carry the meditation experience with you. That you will come slowly out of meditation and enjoy the bliss for an extended period of time. The meditation bliss and peace is much more enjoyable than any sensory experience. You learn to train and discipline the conscious mind, the whole mind and the whole Self. The experiences in meditation; the peace, the bliss, joy, pleasure, fulfillment over time become better than any physical experience you will ever have."

Student: In a good meditation do you experience that peacefulness, bliss, and complete calmness?

"Yes. In a good meditation, you won't go anywhere. You will be everywhere."

Student: I think some students get confused and think that when you meditate some things should be happening.

"Well, they are right. Things should be happening."

Student: But not experiencing astral projection?

"Ah! Meditation and astral projection are two different things. In astral projection you go places. In meditation, you're everywhere. You don't go anywhere, you are everywhere."

Student: I have been taught how to sit in meditation with my spine straight, however, sitting this way is uncomfortable and I have a more difficult time breathing this way. Again, I feel this takes away from meditation experience. Do you have any suggestions?

"Yes. Before you begin meditation do some slow, easy stretching exercises. Also lie flat on your back on a carpeted floor. The firmness of the floor will tend to align your spine. Laying down on the firm surface will also take the pressure off the muscles. Probably you have some vertebrae out of alignment."

Student: If for some reason my meditation is drastically interrupted, is it better to resume and continue right away where I left off, or to start over from the beginning?

"Do not allow your meditation to be drastically interrupted. If you allow yourself to be interrupted then begin again."

Student: At times I love to meditate and feel very peaceful and calm before, during and after—other times it seems to take too much time out of my day—Why do it every day?

"The body and conscious mind work on a 24 hour cycle. One day and one night is 24 hours. The body that houses the soul has followed an evolutionary pattern that has been going on for thousands or millions of years. For true progress to occur within the physical limitations we accepted when we incarned, that must be daily practice and application. This is true whether you wish to become an Olympic athlete or an Olympic meditator."

Student: What is the best way to achieve deeper states of meditation?

"Regular and continual meditation every day, at the same time and in the same place every day. Always having a quiet mind with no thought during meditation so the Self is capable of receiving."

Student: What is meditation?

"The alignment of the Conscious and Subconscious Minds and the gradual or rapid attunement to the Superconscious Mind. This comes from causing the conscious mind to be still so you may listen and be receptive to the Inner Self."

Student: How can I deepen my meditation within 30 to 40 minutes of meditation time?

"By not wasting the first 10 to 20 minutes of your meditation time by getting ready for meditation. When you sit down to meditate, immediately still your mind. Allow no thoughts to run through your head. Approach meditation with the deepest sincerity and gratitude towards your Creator."

Student: How do I carry a meditation through or during physical activity (performing music, voice, instrument, walking, or jogging)?

"By maintaining a focused, quiet, and still mind."

Epilogue

The Secret of Time, Space, Distance and Consciousness

I Am

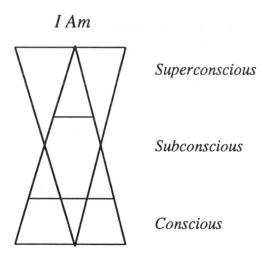

Superconscious

Subconscious

Conscious

In I AM you are everywhere because you are nowhere.

How can this be? What is the meaning to this riddle?

Since I AM is beyond time and space; and Mind is a vehicle of time and space, then when you go beyond Mind to I AM you go beyond time, space, and distance.

In I AM there is no distance between you and me, or any other part of Creation, because we have expanded to fill all Creation. This is called Cosmic Consciousness.

Since there is no distance between us we are everywhere. Since there is no distance we are nowhere and that is the secret meaning to the riddle of Creation and enlightenment.

About the Author

Daniel R. Condron has as his assignment, his commission, for this lifetime to give to the world the understanding of Permanent Healing and the Universal Language of Mind. To achieve either and both these ideals, peace within each individual must be attained.

Meditation is stilling the mind in order to receive from the Divine. From this and following this consciousness can be expanded to experience the Divine in all Creation.

In order for there to be world peace there must be peace within each individual. In meditation you can find lasting and continual peace. This book contains keys to gaining the still mind and inner peace. Dr. Condron has spent over 20 years teaching students to meditate and achieve this expansion of consciousness.

There is something for everyone in this book about meditation. It is his desire that everyone shall achieve Superconscious Meditation.

Daniel R. Condron, D.M., D.D., M.S, Ps.D., was born in Chillicothe, Missouri. Raised on a farm ten miles from that town, he excelled in sports and academics during his high school years. Condron furthered his education at the University of Missouri-Columbia where he earned Bachelors and Masters degrees. He traveled through Europe and South America, and was named to *Who's Who in American Colleges and Universities.*

He has devoted the last thirty years of his life to Self awareness and to understanding the Universal Language of Mind. Serving as a teacher of mind and spirit to people throughout the country, Dr. Condron has shared his knowledge and research with thousands through formal study, seminars and conferences, and all forms of media. His major address on *Permanent Healing - Breakthrough to Awareness* was enthusiastically received at the 1993 Parliament of the World's Religions in Chicago.

Dr. Condron is Chancellor of the College of Metaphysics which is the University of the World for Intuitive Man (thinker). He serves as President of the Board of Directors of the School of Metaphysics, an educational and service institute with centers throughout the United States and headquartered in Missouri. His influence continues to reach around the globe as a conductor of intuitive reports including the Intuitive Health Analyses, offered through the institute. For his innovations as a teacher and world server he is recognized in current editions of *Who'sWho in America* and *Who'sWho in the World.*

Dr. Condron looks forward to aiding millions more people to create and lead a richer, and more fulfilling life.

Additional titles available from SOM Publishing include:

The Universal Language of Mind
The Book of Matthew Interpreted
Dr. Daniel R. Condron   ISBN 0944386-15-6 $13.00

Permanent Healing
Dr. Daniel R. Condron   ISBN 0944386-12-1 $13.00

Dreams of the Soul
The Yogi Sutras of Patanjali
Dr. Daniel R. Condron   ISBN 0944386-11-3 $9.95

The Dreamer's Dictionary
Dr. Barbara Condron   ISBN 0944386-16-4 $15.00

First Opinion
Wholistic Health Care in the 21st Century
Dr. Barbara Condron, ed.   ISBN 0944386-18-0 $15.00

The Work of the Soul
Past Life Recall & Spiritual Enlightenment
Dr. Barbara Condron, ed.   ISBN 0944386-17-2 $13.00

Uncommon Knowledge
Past Life & Health Readings
Dr. Barbara Condron, ed.   ISBN 0944386-19-9 $13.00

Kundalini Rising
Mastering Your Creative Energies
Dr. Barbara Condron   ISBN 0944386-13-X $13.00

Spiritual Guide to Visualization
Laurel Fuller Clark ISBN 0944386-14-8 $13.00

Going in Circles
Our Search for a Satisfying Relationship
Dr. Barbara Condron ISBN 0944386-00-8 $5.95

What Will I Do Tomorrow? Probing Depression
Dr. Barbara Condron ISBN 0944386-02-4 $4.95

Who Were Those Strangers in My Dream?
Dr. Barbara Condron ISBN 0944386-08-3 $4.95

Discovering the Kingdom of Heaven
Dr. Gayle B. Matthes ISBN 0944386-07-5 $5.95

To order write:

School of Metaphysics
World Headquarters
HCR 1, Box 15
Windyville, Missouri 65783
U.S.A.

Enclose a check or money order payable in U.S. funds to SOM with any order. Please include $3.00 for postage and handling of books, $6 for international orders.

A complete catalogue of all book titles, audio lectures and courses, and videos is available upon request.

Visit us on the Internet at *http://www.som.org*

About the School of Metaphysics

We invite you to become a special part of our efforts to aid in enhancing and quickening the process of spiritual growth and mental evolution of the people of the world. The School of Metaphysics, a not-for-profit educational and service organization, has been in existence for more than two decades. During that time, we have taught tens of thousands directly through our course of study in applied metaphysics. We have elevated the awareness of millions through the many services we offer. If you would like to pursue the study of mind and the transformation of Self to a higher level of being and consciousness, you are invited to write to us at the School of Metaphysics World Headquarters in Windyville, Missouri 65783.

The heart of the School of Metaphysics is a three-tiered program of study. Lessons introduce you to the Universal Laws and Truths which guide spiritual and physical evolution. Consciousness is explored and developed through mental and spiritual disciplines which enhance your physical life and enrich your soul progression. We teach concentration, visualization (focused imagery), meditation, and control of life force and creative energies. As a student, you will develop an understanding of the purpose of life and your purpose for this lifetime.

Experts in the Universal Language of Mind, we teach how to remember and understand the inner communication received through dreams. We are the sponsors of the National Dream Hotline®, an annual educational service offered the last weekend in April. Study centers are located throughout the Midwestern United States. If there is not a center near you, you can receive the first series of lessons through correspondence with a teacher at our headquarters.

For those desiring spiritual renewal, weekends at our Moon Valley Ranch offer calmness and clarity. Each Spiritual Initiation Session's mentor gives thematic instruction and guidance which enriches the Spirit and changes lives. One weekend may center on transcendent meditation, another on creative genius, another on wholistic health or understanding your dreams. Please feel free to contact us about upcoming sessions.

The Universal Hour of Peace was initiated by the School of Metaphysics at noon Universal Time (GMT) on October 24, 1995 in conjunction with the 50th anniversary of the United Nations. We believe that peace on earth is an idea whose time has come. To realize this dream, we invite you to join with others throughout the world by dedicating your thoughts and actions to peace for one hour beginning at noon [UT] on the first of January each year. Living peaceably begins by thinking peacefully. We invite SOMA® members to convene Circles of Love in their cities during this hour. Please contact us about how you can participate.

There is the opportunity to aid in the growth and fulfillment of our work. Donations supporting the expansion of the School of Metaphysics' efforts are a valuable way for you to aid humanity. As a not-for-profit publishing house, SOM Publishing is dedicated to the continuing publication of research findings that promote peace, under-standing and good will for all of Mankind. It is dependent upon the kindness and generosity of sponsors to do so. Authors donate their work and receive no royalties. We have many excellent manuscripts awaiting a benefactor.

One hundred percent of the donations made to the School of Metaphysics are used to expand our services. Donations are being received for Project Octagon, the first educational building on the College of Metaphysics campus. The land for the proposed campus is located in the beautiful Ozark Mountains of Missouri. This proposed multipurpose structure will include an auditorium, classrooms, library and study areas, a cafeteria, and potential living quarters for up to 100 people. We expect to finance this structure through corporate grants and personal endowments. Donations to the School of Metaphysics are tax-exempt under 501 (c) (3) of the Internal Revenue Code. We appreciate any contribution you are free to make. With the help of people like you, our dream of a place where anyone desiring Self awareness can receive wholistic education will become a reality.

We send you our Circle of Love.